The Best-Ever Boo
FLIGHT

Ian Graham

KINGFISHER
Kingfisher Publications Plc
New Penderel House,
283–288 High Holborn,
London WC1V 7HZ
www.kingfisherpub.com

First published by Kingfisher Publications Plc 2001
10 9 8 7 6 5 4 3 2 1 (hb)
1TR/0501/GCUP/MA/157MA

First published in paperback 2003
10 9 8 7 6 5 4 3 2 1 (pb)
1TR/0203/GCUP/MA/128NMA

A CIP catalogue record for this book is available from the
British Library.

ISBN 0 7534 0531 8 (hb)
ISBN 0 7534 0632 2 (pb)

Senior editor: Clive Wilson
Art director: Mike Davis
Production controller: Debbie Otter
DTP manager: Nicky Studdart
Picture manager: Jane Lambert
Indexer: Hilary Bird

The Publisher would like to thank the Royal Aeronautical
Society for their help and co-operation in the production
of this book. Further information about the Society can
be obtained from its website: www.aerosociety.com

All views expressed are the author's own.

Printed in China

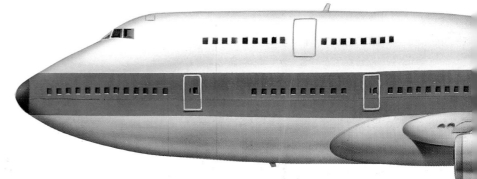

CONTENTS

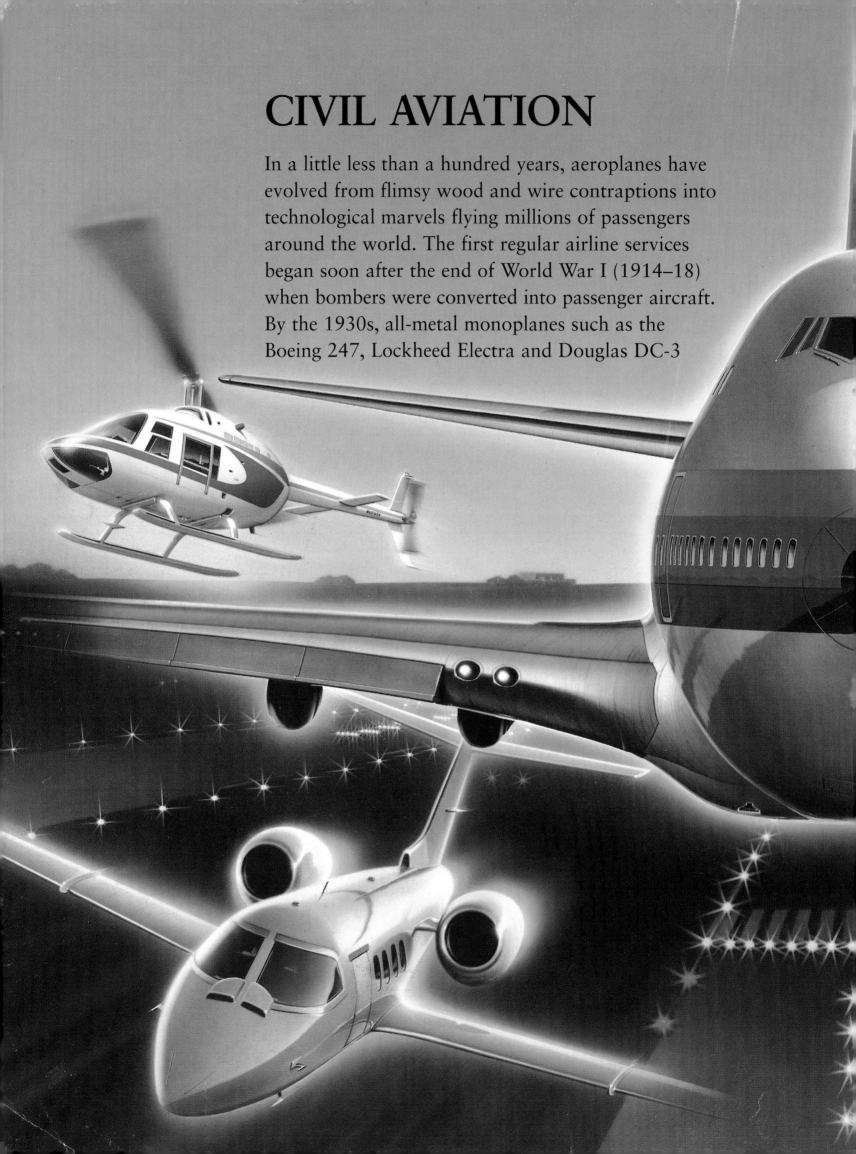

CIVIL AVIATION

In a little less than a hundred years, aeroplanes have evolved from flimsy wood and wire contraptions into technological marvels flying millions of passengers around the world. The first regular airline services began soon after the end of World War I (1914–18) when bombers were converted into passenger aircraft. By the 1930s, all-metal monoplanes such as the Boeing 247, Lockheed Electra and Douglas DC-3

were much faster and more comfortable for those who could afford air travel. The first jet airliner, the British de Havilland DH106 Comet, which had 44 seats, entered service in 1952. The first US jet airliner, the 147-seater Boeing 707, flew five years later and helped to make air travel affordable and popular. At the end of the 1960s, a new type of airliner – the wide-bodied jet – was introduced. Today, there is a huge range of commercial aircraft from small business jets and helicopters to the massive Boeing 747-400.

Herald of a new age
The first modern airliner was the Boeing 247, which was introduced in 1933. It was a metal monoplane with retractable wheels and an enclosed cabin with seats for 10 passengers.

Airliners

Every day, thousands of airliners criss-cross the skies. They include tiny island hoppers and commuter planes, with room for only a few passengers, as well as some of the world's largest aircraft, which can carry over 400 passengers. One of these, the Boeing 747 'Jumbo Jet', has flown more than 1.8 billion passengers over 40 billion kilometres since it was first introduced in 1969. These airliners are so enormous that the Wright brothers' first-ever aeroplane flight could have been flown inside one!

Sky trains
During the 1920s, air travellers sat in passenger cabins that often looked like luxury railway carriages – which is how wealthy passengers were used to travelling. Aeroplanes flew in the rough air below 5,000 metres, much lower than they do today, so flights could be very uncomfortable.

Jumbo-size
The biggest airliner currently in service is the Boeing 747-400. It has a maximum capacity of up to 568 people, although it typically carries 420 passengers. This massive aircraft is 70 metres long, has a wingspan of 64 metres and can weigh up to 395 tonnes at take-off.

A breath of fresh air

Airliners cruise at a height of about 13,000 metres. At this altitude, the air can be as cold as -60°C and too thin to breathe. However, airline passengers don't have to wear oxygen masks like fighter pilots. Air entering the engines is compressed before it flows into the combustion chambers where the fuel is burned. Compressing the air makes it thick enough to breathe, but also heats it up to about 350°C. Refrigeration units cool some of this air down and then feed it inside the aeroplane for the crew and passengers to breathe.

Twentieth-century classic

Although it was designed as an airliner, the Lockheed Constellation first saw service as a military transporter during World War II. After the war, it was re-converted to an airliner. The 'Connie' had beautiful curving lines and a distinctive triple-fin tail. Early models carried up to 60 passengers. Bigger versions were built well into the 1950s.

Faster than sound

In 1976, a revolutionary new airliner took to the skies. Concorde was the first civil aeroplane that could fly faster than sound. Concorde represented a huge leap forward in airliner technology. Cruising at 2,150km/h, or more than twice the speed of sound, it slashed long-distance flight times in half. A subsonic airliner flies from London to New York in about seven hours. Concorde could fly the same route in only 3.5 hours. Even the most advanced fighter-planes could not match Concorde's performance.

Glamorous Glennis
Charles 'Chuck' Yeager stands beside the Bell *X-1* rocket-plane. On October 14, 1947, Yeager made the first-ever supersonic flight in the *X-1*. He reached a speed of 1,126km/h. The record-breaking plane was named *Glamorous Glennis* after Yeager's wife.

Sonic booms
As Concorde accelerates through the speed of sound, air piles up in front of it, forming a shock wave. A second shock wave forms at the tail. The shock waves reach the ground, making a double bang, or sonic boom, as they pass over.

Future Concordes
Aircraft manufacturers are designing new supersonic airliners. Computer simulations are used to study the way air flows around them (right). Concorde's successor will be bigger, quieter and powered by engines that are less harmful to the environment.

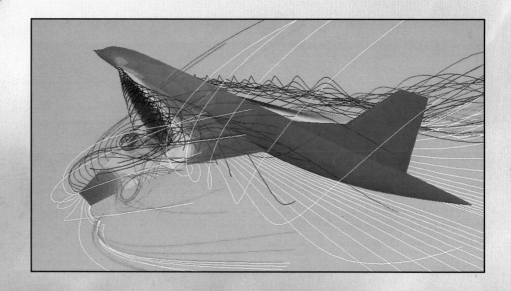

Nose of distinction
Concorde's distinctive nose is pointed so that it can punch through the air at twice the speed of sound.

As Concorde begins its descent prior to landing, its visor slides down into the nose to reveal the cockpit's windshield.

Finally, the nose itself is lowered to give the crew a better view of the ground. This nose-down position is also used for take-off.

Supersonic powerplants
At full power, Concorde's engines generate 70 tonnes of thrust, more than twice the maximum thrust of the biggest Jumbo Jet. During a flight across the Atlantic Ocean, its four Rolls-Royce/SNECMA Olympus jet engines burn about 80 tonnes of fuel.

Tough tyres
Concorde's speed at take-off is 400km/h. This is faster than any other airliner – a Boeing 747, for example, takes off at 320 km/h. Concorde's tyres have to be immensely strong and to make the rubber extra tough, it is reinforced with steel cables. If a tyre should burst, the pieces can damage the aircraft. In July 2000, a tyre bursting on take-off probably caused an Air France Concorde to crash, killing everyone on board. All Concordes were grounded while designers and engineers investigated ways of preventing a similar tragedy happening again.

Building an airliner

Airliners are among the most complex machines ever built and they are assembled inside some of the largest buildings on Earth. The main Boeing Jumbo Jet production hall at Everett in Washington, USA, is 600 metres wide and nearly 500 metres long – the equivalent of 25 full-size football pitches! Each plane is made from up to six million parts. More than 10,000 people work round the clock to produce about five Jumbo Jets in a month. When each one has been built, the seating and paint scheme ordered by the airline complete the job. Finally, the aeroplane is ready to be flight-tested and then delivered to the airline.

The assembly hall
Airbus airliners (*main picture*) are made in sections by 30,000 workers all over Europe. The cockpit and centre section of the aircraft are made in France, the rest of the fuselage in Germany, the tail in Spain and the wings in Britain. Engines come from Britain and the United States. The sections are joined together and the aircraft are completed in a cavernous hangar in Toulouse, France.

Close inspection

Airlines and their pilots are closely involved in the development of a new airliner. They are invited to inspect mock-ups and prototypes of the new aircraft.

New for old

Airliners undergo regular maintenance and servicing. Every part of the aeroplane has a built-in life expectancy, so that it can be replaced before it breaks down. Depending on the type of aircraft, an airliner is completely rebuilt every four to eight years. It is taken apart and stripped down to the bare metal. Any faulty parts are repaired or replaced. Then, the aeroplane is put back together again and repainted. The whole process can take up to three months.

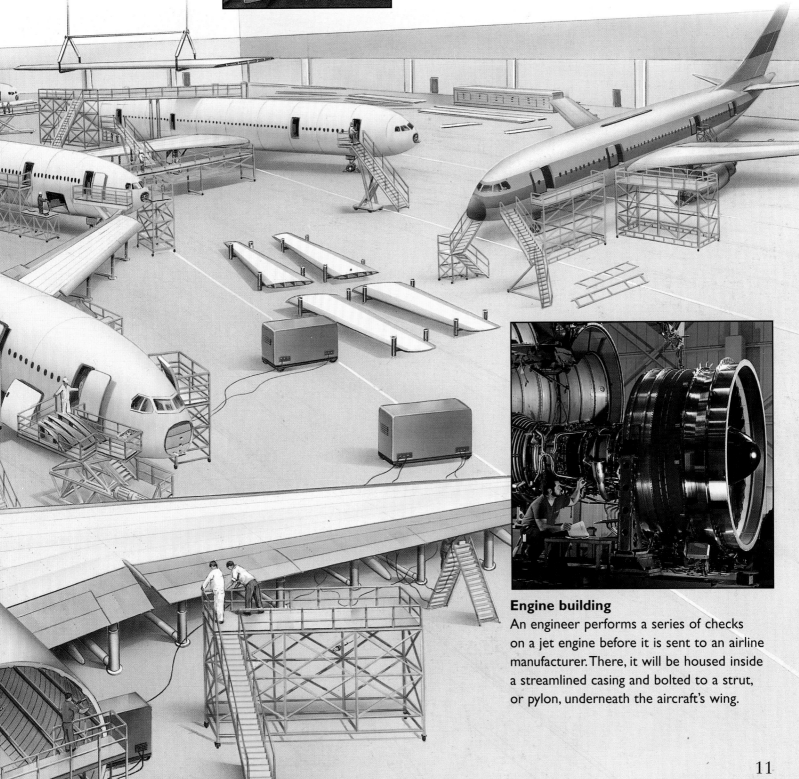

Engine building
An engineer performs a series of checks on a jet engine before it is sent to an airline manufacturer. There, it will be housed inside a streamlined casing and bolted to a strut, or pylon, underneath the aircraft's wing.

Spinning blades

The idea of building a craft that flies vertically up into the air dates back to the 1300s. But it took another 600 years before the technology became available to make this a reality with the invention of the helicopter. Instead of wings, helicopters have long, thin rotor blades. When they spin, the blades cut through the air and create lift even when the helicopter itself is not moving forwards. This allows helicopters to fly in ways that are impossible for fixed-wing aircraft. Their ability to take off vertically, fly in any direction and hover makes them ideal for all kinds of tasks. Helicopters are often used for rescue work, military transport and flying passengers to and from tiny city centre heliports.

The tiltrotor
The tiltrotor can fly like a fixed-wing craft but can take off and land like a helicopter. It has wings and very large propellers called proprotors.

As a tiltrotor comes in to land, its engines slowly tilt up. The proprotors start to provide some of the lift instead of the wings.

The aircraft slows down and, with the engines pointing straight upwards, it can hover and land in a confined space, just like a helicopter.

Leonardo da Vinci
The Italian artist and scientist Leonardo da Vinci (1452-1519) made one of the earliest drawings of a helicopter in about 1500. His sketch shows a design for an air-screw, or corkscrew propeller. He thought the device would spin up into the air when the air-screw turned.

Speed restrictions

Helicopters pay a price for their amazing flying abilities – they cannot fly as fast as fixed-wing aircraft. Whirling rotor blades create much more air resistance than a smooth thin wing. Also, a high proportion of the engine power has to produce lift instead of propelling the aircraft through the air. As a result, most helicopters fly at just 200-300km/h compared to 500-700km/h for a small twin-engine turboprop aircraft. However, a new type of aircraft called a tiltrotor overcomes this by using long propellers that also work as rotors. A tiltrotor takes off vertically and it can hover, like a helicopter. Its engines then swing forwards and the rotors become propellers. A tiltrotor can fly at speeds up to 500km/h.

Flood rescue

A Kawasaki BK117 helicopter winches people to safety from a tree-top during the disastrous floods that swamped large parts of Mozambique in February 2000. The water rose so fast that there was little time to escape and thousands of people were trapped on roofs and in tree-tops. Helicopters were the only aircraft that could reach them quickly.

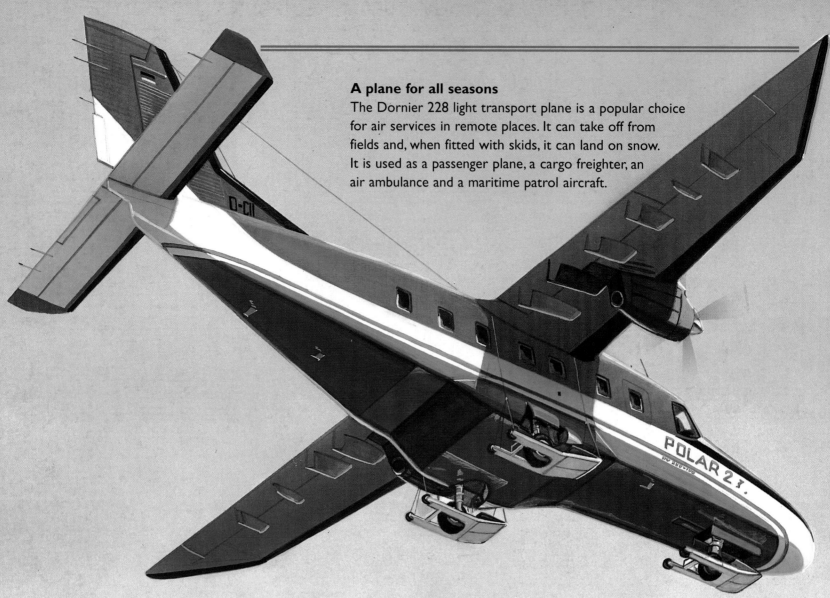

A plane for all seasons
The Dornier 228 light transport plane is a popular choice for air services in remote places. It can take off from fields and, when fitted with skids, it can land on snow. It is used as a passenger plane, a cargo freighter, an air ambulance and a maritime patrol aircraft.

To the ends of the Earth

In many of the remotest parts of the world, the only practical way to get around is by air. Communities on the polar ice caps and in the Australian outback, for example, depend on aircraft for essential supplies and emergency services. Even more isolated are offshore oil rigs or gas platforms. These rely mainly on helicopters to ferry workers to and from the mainland and to carry supplies. Each rig has a helipad, or a platform where helicopters land. Amphibious aircraft, which can land on water, are particularly useful in places like Canada, where there are lakes and rivers on which to land. Seaplanes also provide air-links between far-flung islands.

Flying doctors
The huge distances between homes in the Australian outback mean that often the only way to get medical help quickly to people is by air. In 1928, Rev J. Flynn founded the Royal Flying Doctor Service, which uses light planes to fly doctors to wherever they are needed.

Flexible flyers

Aircraft that fly to remote places are chosen because of their special capabilities or modified to cope with extreme conditions. Short Take-Off and Landing (STOL) planes are often used because they can take off from and land on very short runways or landing fields. They are sometimes fitted with extra fuel tanks because they may not be able to re-fuel where they land. Aircraft flying to the polar wastes are fitted with skids or skis to spread their weight over a larger area and stop them from sinking into the snow.

Going home
A Sikorsky S-61N Sea King transport helicopter takes off from an oil rig's helipad, carrying oil workers home to the mainland for a well-earned break. The Sea King's watertight, boat-shaped body enables it to land on water in an emergency.

Fighting fires
The Canadair CL-415 is a twin-engined amphibious plane. Its boat-shaped hull and floats under the wings enable it to land on water. It also has wheels for landing on a runway. The CL-415 was designed as a fire-fighting aircraft to protect Canada's forests. While skimming a lake, it can take 6,000 litres of water on-board in only 12 seconds.

FLYING FOR FUN

In the early days of aviation, flying circuses thrilled the crowds. Air races also proved to be an exciting sport for pilots and spectators and helped to speed up the development of aircraft technology. The flying circuses have gone, but air races are still held and they are as closely fought as ever. Aerobatics have grown in popularity because of the amazing manoeuvres the pilots can perform. As commercial aviation developed in the 1950s and 60s, so did sport and leisure flying. Elegant gliders, small piston-engine aircraft, thoroughbred racers and nimble aerobatic planes were built and flown in increasing numbers. The variety of aircraft available for sport and leisure flying has never been greater. Microlights and hang-gliders enable almost anyone to enjoy the thrill of flight, while new technology is giving the earliest types of aircraft a new lease of life. The oldest of all, hot-air balloons, have become popular again and airships, the first aircraft to offer luxury air travel, are taking to the skies again.

Aerial sports

Pilots can compete against each other in two ways – racing and aerobatics. In the early years of aviation, air races helped to encourage the development of new, faster planes. Pilots could win valuable prize money and trophies. In 1920, the winner of the Schneider Trophy flew at 172 km/h, while the 1931 winner reached a top speed of 547 km/h. Today, the US National Championship Air Races are held near Reno, Nevada, USA. Aerobatic contests are less concerned with speed than flying skills. Pilots fly one at a time, or in teams, making their planes tumble and roll in carefully planned manoeuvres.

Roll over
The Pitts Special is a very popular choice for aerobatics and stunt flying. Its short fuselage and biplane wings make it a very strong and agile performer. With a flick of the joystick, the pilot can roll the aircraft all the way round in just over one second!

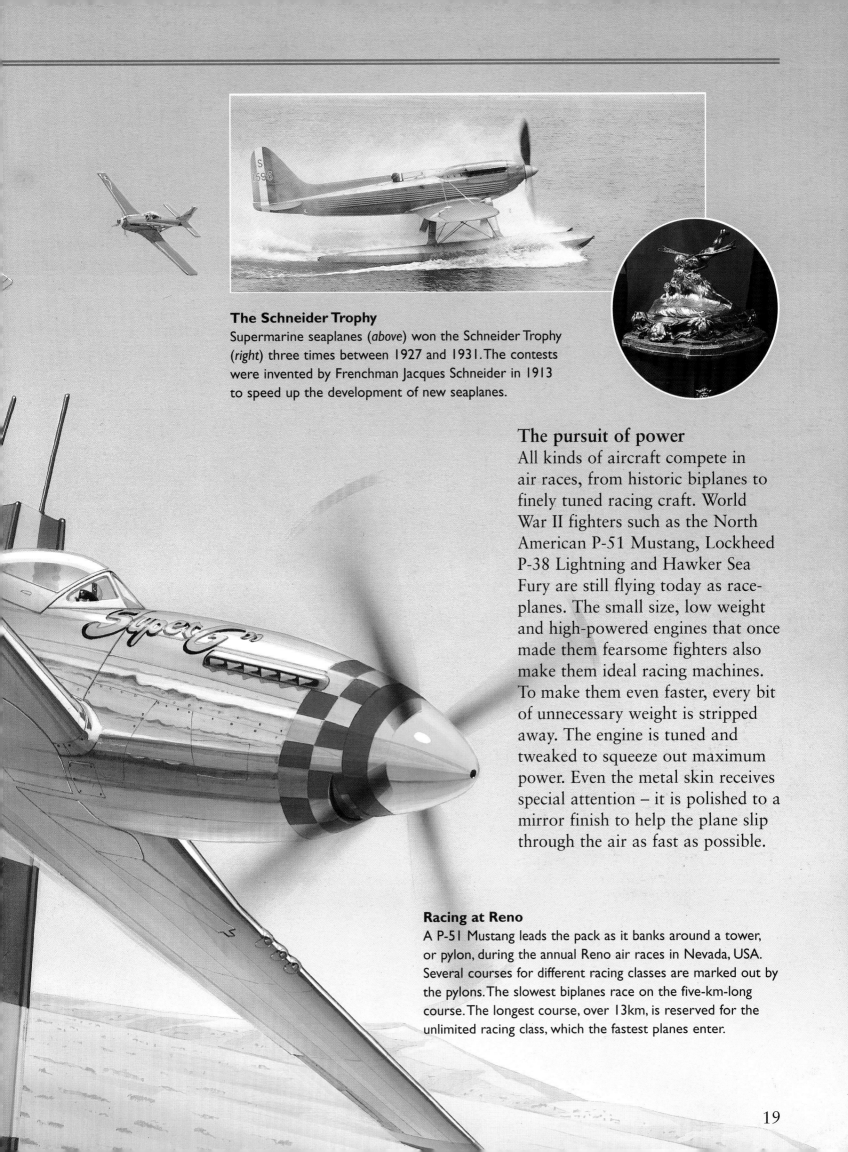

The Schneider Trophy
Supermarine seaplanes (*above*) won the Schneider Trophy (*right*) three times between 1927 and 1931. The contests were invented by Frenchman Jacques Schneider in 1913 to speed up the development of new seaplanes.

The pursuit of power
All kinds of aircraft compete in air races, from historic biplanes to finely tuned racing craft. World War II fighters such as the North American P-51 Mustang, Lockheed P-38 Lightning and Hawker Sea Fury are still flying today as race-planes. The small size, low weight and high-powered engines that once made them fearsome fighters also make them ideal racing machines. To make them even faster, every bit of unnecessary weight is stripped away. The engine is tuned and tweaked to squeeze out maximum power. Even the metal skin receives special attention – it is polished to a mirror finish to help the plane slip through the air as fast as possible.

Racing at Reno
A P-51 Mustang leads the pack as it banks around a tower, or pylon, during the annual Reno air races in Nevada, USA. Several courses for different racing classes are marked out by the pylons. The slowest biplanes race on the five-km-long course. The longest course, over 13km, is reserved for the unlimited racing class, which the fastest planes enter.

Light aircraft and gliders

Light aircraft are the taxis of the aviation world. With room for three or four passengers and a top speed of no more than 300km/h, they are ideal for short flights of up to 1,000km. As well as leisure flights by private pilots, they carry tourists on sight-seeing tours and are often used as air ambulances. The lightest aircraft of all are microlights, ultralights, hang-gliders and gliders. Gliders and hang-gliders are generally unpowered. They soar on rising currents of air, which their pilots become expert in detecting. Fun to fly, light aircraft give thousands of people their first taste of piloting an aircraft.

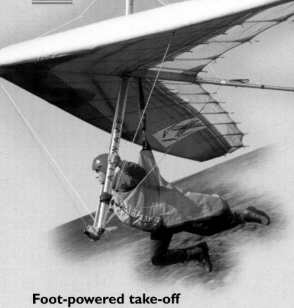

Foot-powered take-off
A hang-glider pilot takes to the air. This type of hang-glider has a stiff wing. Others are made from a metal frame covered with flexible material that billows into a wing shape when filled with air. A pilot turns a hang-glider to the left or right by shifting his or her weight to one side. Speed can be controlled by tipping the wing up or down.

Air tourism
A Piper PA-23 Aztec gives its passengers a bird's-eye view of the Grand Canyon in Arizona, USA. The twin-engine Aztec has been providing air taxi, leisure, tourism and business services for 30 years and it is still widely used today for training new pilots.

Micro-seaplanes

A microlight seaplane prepares for landing. The pilot sits in an open cockpit and flies the plane with the same stick and pedal controls that are used by other light aircraft.

Light and manoeuvrable

Microlights are small, low-cost, lightweight powered craft. There are two main types of microlight – weightshift and three-axis control. Weightshift craft are steered by the pilot shifting his or her weight in the same way as a hang-glider pilot. Three-axis craft have flying controls like larger aircraft. They may have an enclosed cockpit and there are even float-plane and flying boat versions for landing on water. The lightest type of microlight is a powered parachute. This is a long, slender, wing-shaped parachute powered by an engine and propeller which are strapped to the pilot hanging underneath it.

Thermals

Gliders can climb by circling inside rising air. Air rises when it is warmed by land that has been heated by the Sun and when wind is deflected upwards by hills. Rising columns of warm air are called thermals.

Soaring in silence

Gliders are made of strong but lightweight materials such as glass-reinforced plastic. Once a glider has been launched – either by catapult from the ground or by towing it aloft – it can stay airborne for many hours.

Lighter than air

Airships and balloons are able to fly because they are lighter than the air around them, even though they are made from materials that are heavier than air. They manage this seemingly impossible task by carrying a huge bag full of lighter-than-air gas. The lifting force, or buoyancy, of the gas overcomes the craft's weight and it floats upwards. Most airships use helium, a non-flammable gas, while most balloons use hot air, which is lighter than cold air.

Historic day
The first manned flight in an untethered craft was made in November 1783. Pilâtre de Rozier and the Marquis d'Arlandes drifted across Paris in a hot-air balloon built by Étienne and Joseph Montgolfier.

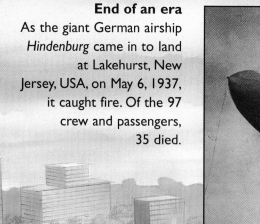

Hot and cold
A hot-air balloon's height is controlled by burning gas to heat up the air inside it. This creates lift. To descend, hot air is released through a vent and replaced by cooler, heavier air.

Fire hazards
Airships are lighter-than-air powered craft that can be steered. During the 1920s and 1930s, they flew passengers in great comfort and style across oceans and continents. However, there was always the risk of fire as most airships were filled with hydrogen which catches alight very easily. A series of disasters during the 1930s, as well as the beginning of World War II in 1939, ended the age of passenger airship travel. Today, airships are making a comeback using helium, a much safer gas than hydrogen.

End of an era
As the giant German airship *Hindenburg* came in to land at Lakehurst, New Jersey, USA, on May 6, 1937, it caught fire. Of the 97 crew and passengers, 35 died.

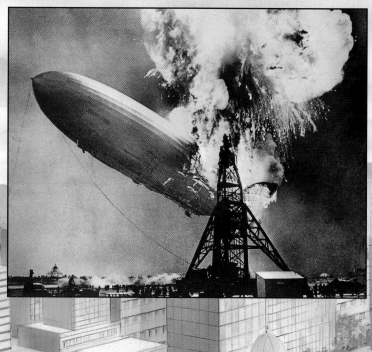

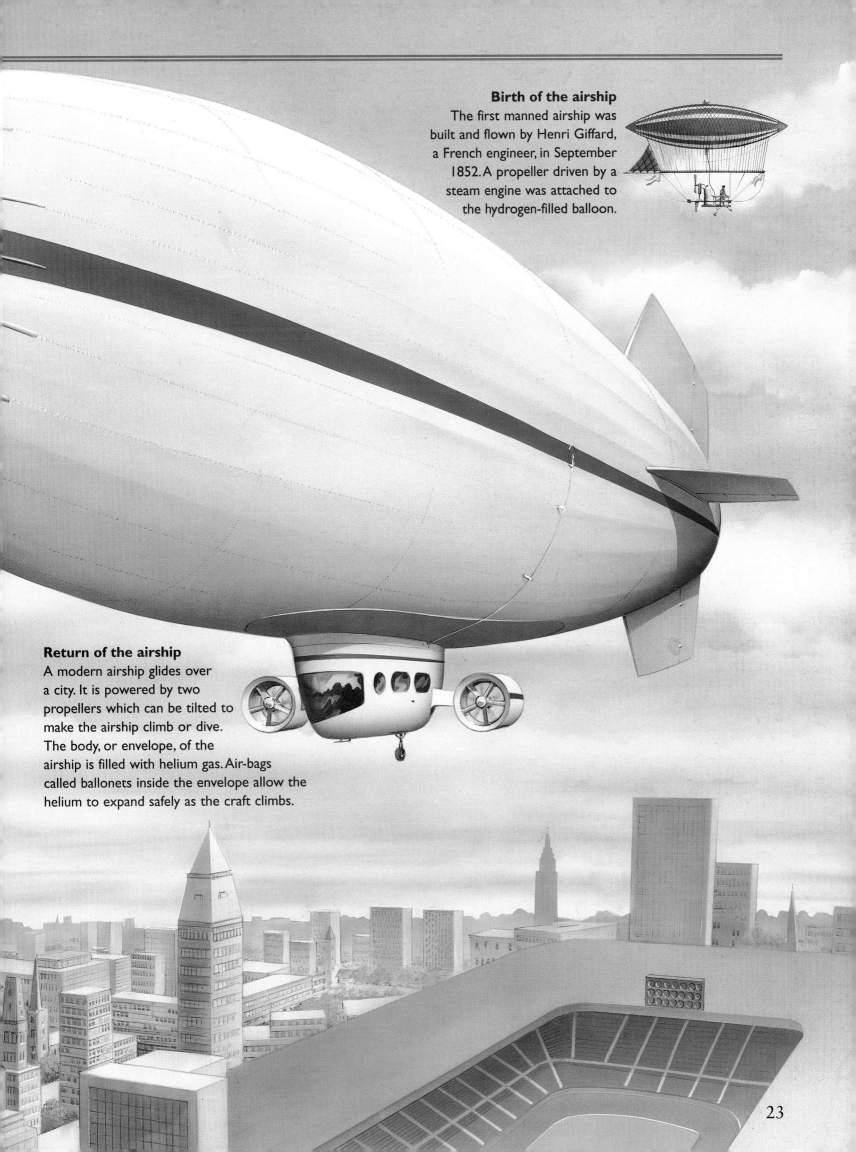

Birth of the airship
The first manned airship was built and flown by Henri Giffard, a French engineer, in September 1852. A propeller driven by a steam engine was attached to the hydrogen-filled balloon.

Return of the airship
A modern airship glides over a city. It is powered by two propellers which can be tilted to make the airship climb or dive. The body, or envelope, of the airship is filled with helium gas. Air-bags called ballonets inside the envelope allow the helium to expand safely as the craft climbs.

AIR SAFETY

Safety is the top priority at every stage of aircraft design, manufacture and operation. International safety regulations ensure that air travel is one of the safest forms of transport. The most important on-board systems are duplicated so that if one fails in flight, there is at least one back-up, and usually more than one, to take over. On-board computers quickly detect faults and alert the crew. If an aircraft develops a serious problem, safety equipment ranging from oxygen masks and life jackets to escape chutes and fire fighting systems help to protect the crew and passengers. Combat aircraft also have ejector seats to let crews escape quickly.

On the ground, air traffic controllers play a crucial part in air safety by making sure that aircraft remain a safe distance apart. On the very rare occasions when a plane crashes, the causes are investigated and analyzed in great detail to help prevent similar crashes happening again.

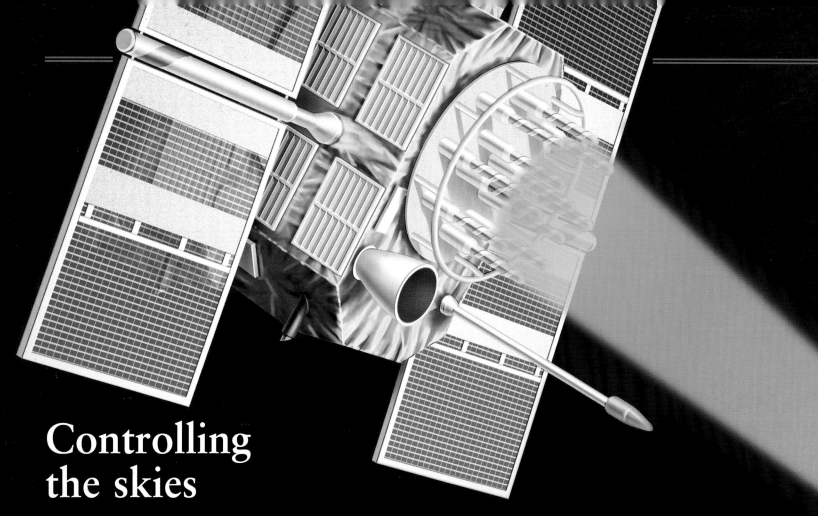

Controlling the skies

An airliner's crew steers a course by using radio signals from beacons on the ground and satellites orbiting the Earth. Air traffic controllers track aircraft movements and give the crew permission to change height and direction when necessary. The controllers are able to see exactly where the aircraft are by using radar. This uses radio waves reflected by an aircraft to show its position on a radar screen. Each plane transmits information about itself and this also appears on the screen.

GPS satellite
Aircraft can locate their position using GPS satellites. Each satellite orbits the Earth every 12 hours at a height of 18,000km. Solar panels generate 800 watts of electricity to power its communications equipment.

Ground control
An airliner's movements are directed by air traffic controllers from the moment it leaves the terminal building. Aircraft on the ground are guided from the airport's visual control room, a room with large windows in the control tower overlooking the runways.

Satellite navigation

Airliners pinpoint their position by measuring the direction to radio beacons (transmitters) in known positions on the ground. However, there are large parts of the world where there are no radio beacons, so most airliners now also use a satellite navigation system that covers the whole world. The Global Positioning System (GPS) consists of 24 satellites orbiting the Earth. Using radio signals transmitted by any four satellites, an airliner can find its position very accurately.

Flying by eye

In the early years of aviation, aircraft rarely flew out of sight of land, so pilots could steer a course by using a map and compass. They also followed well-known landmarks on the ground such as rivers, towns, railways, valleys and coastlines.

Skyways

Airliners can fly automatically from one place to another, using navigation satellites and beacons to update their flight computers. Aeroplanes fly through invisible airways, or 'air corridors', 18km wide and 300m apart vertically.

Air hazards

All forms of transport involve some level of risk. Aircraft, just like other complicated machines, can occasionally break down. In addition to mechanical or electrical problems, such as engine failure and fires, aircraft are also affected by extreme weather such as storms and lightning. They run the risk of collisions and terrorist attacks. However, the hazards involved in air travel are well known and dealt with so effectively that accidents are very rare. Statistically, you would have to fly for 2,000 million kilometres before becoming a victim of a fatal accident.

Comet catastrophe
When three de Havilland Comets, the world's first jet airliner (*top*), crashed in 1953 and 1954, all Comets were grounded. Air crash investigators pumped a Comet full of water again and again (*above*) to simulate the effect of air pressure during a flight. The fuselage cracked open, revealing that metal fatigue was the cause of the accidents.

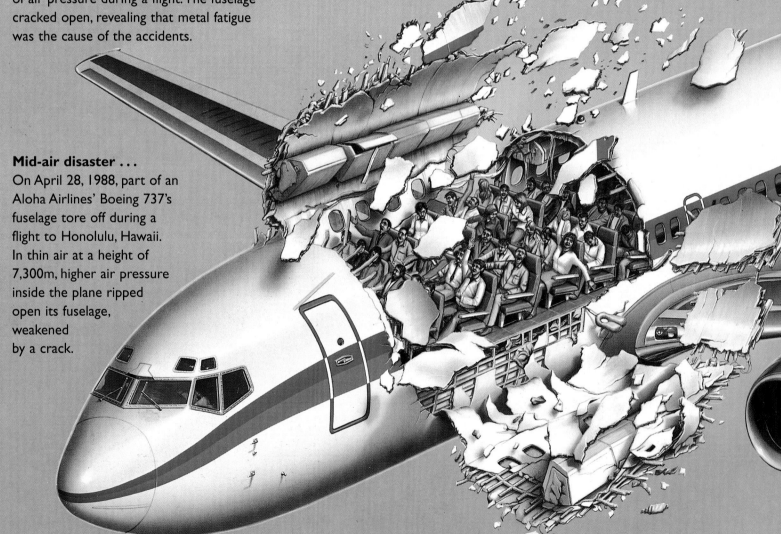

Mid-air disaster ...
On April 28, 1988, part of an Aloha Airlines' Boeing 737's fuselage tore off during a flight to Honolulu, Hawaii. In thin air at a height of 7,300m, higher air pressure inside the plane ripped open its fuselage, weakened by a crack.

Windshear

A sudden change in wind direction or speed, called windshear, can rob a plane of lift and height. This is very dangerous when a plane is near the ground and can result in a crash. Windshear is often caused by downward wind from a rainstorm called a microburst. Airliners now have windshear warning systems on board.

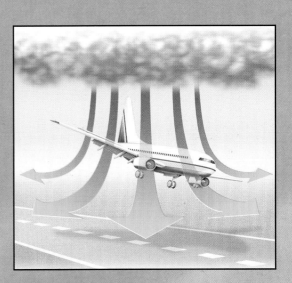

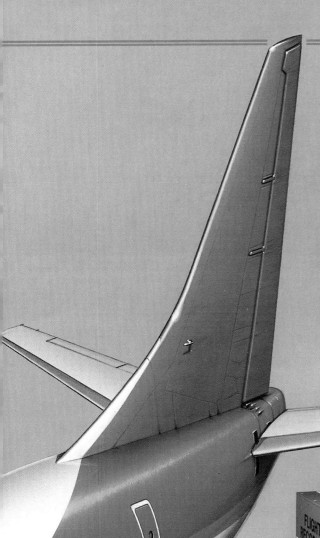

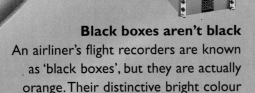

Black boxes aren't black
An airliner's flight recorders are known as 'black boxes', but they are actually orange. Their distinctive bright colour makes them much easier to find.

Flight recorders

Large airliners carry two machines that record information about the plane and the way it flies. The flight data recorder records information including the plane's height, speed, direction, pitch (how much its nose is tipped up or down) and how fast it is climbing or diving. The cockpit voice recorder records the last half-hour of the crew's voices and other sounds on the flight deck. In the event of a crash, these recorders provide vital clues to why the accident happened. The recorders are built to survive a crash, fire and immersion in water.

... Safe landing
Passengers are evacuated from Aloha Airlines Flight 243 immediately after its emergency arrival at Kahului Airport on the Hawaiian Island of Maui. Even though the plane was so badly damaged, the crew was able to make a normal landing. Of the 95 people aboard, one flight attendant died.

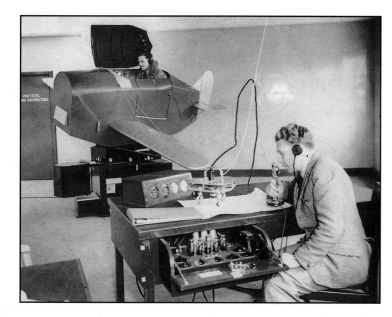

Blind flying

By the 1930s, aircraft instruments gave pilots enough information to fly without the need to look outside. However, it was very dangerous for pilots to practise 'blind flying', as this is called, in real aircraft. Early flight simulators, such as this one, were used to teach blind flying in safety.

Flight simulators

Pilots are trained to cope with every imaginable situation. They rehearse in-flight emergencies again and again. And they can do it without ever actually leaving the ground, by using flight simulators. A flight simulator is an exact copy of the inside of real plane's cockpit. The pilot looks out at a computer-generated view and experiences every movement as if he or she is really flying. Flight simulators teach pilots how to deal with dangerous situations without risking real aircraft. They are also much less expensive than taking airliners out of service for training flights.

Virtual flying

Modern flight simulators stand on computer-controlled legs. They tilt the simulator in different directions to give pilots the sensation of flying. The pilots are cut off from the real world. They see, hear and feel only the virtual world created by the computer.

Going nowhere

A training officer sits at a control desk behind the pilots inside a Boeing 747-400 flight simulator. It is identical to the 747-400's flight deck. The trainer can test the crew's skills by re-creating a huge range of different conditions, from bad weather to potentially catastrophic faults in the aircraft.

Digital airports

A flight simulator's computer system is programmed with digital copies of the world's major airports. So, when a simulator crew approaches Hong Kong or New York, they see what appears to be the real landscape and airport. The training officer can make things more difficult for them by adding fog, cross-winds, windshear. rain, or dozens of other weather effects and any of 500 different equipment failures. In fact, flight simulators are so good that pilots can qualify to fly aircraft before ever flying the real plane itself.

Going nowhere

A training officer sits at a control desk behind the pilots inside a Boeing 747-400 flight simulator. It is identical to the 747-400's flight deck. The trainer can test the crew's skills by re-creating a huge range of different conditions, from bad weather to potentially catastrophic faults in the aircraft.

Digital airports

A flight simulator's computer system is programmed with digital copies of the world's major airports. So, when a simulator crew approaches Hong Kong or New York, they see what appears to be the real landscape and airport. The training officer can make things more difficult for them by adding fog, cross-winds, windshear. rain, or dozens of other weather effects and any of 500 different equipment failures. In fact, flight simulators are so good that pilots can qualify to fly aircraft before ever flying the real plane itself.

AIR POWER

Air power is a vital part of modern warfare. Controlling the skies over a war zone is frequently the key to winning the ground war. Aircraft went to war only eight years after the Wright brothers made the first powered flight. In 1911, Italian forces used a Blériot plane to spy on Turkish troops in North Africa. During World War I (1914–1918), new kinds of warplane were designed and built, including fighters, bombers, transport planes and ground attack aircraft. When helicopters were developed in the 1930s, they provided military forces with a new type of weapon. Today, there are warplanes that can fly at more than twice the speed of sound, stealth planes that can fly to their targets without being detected and transport planes big enough to carry more than 100 tonnes of cargo.

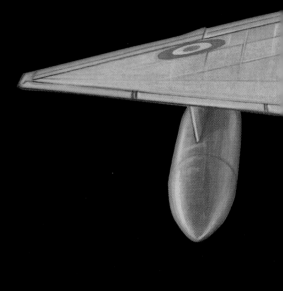

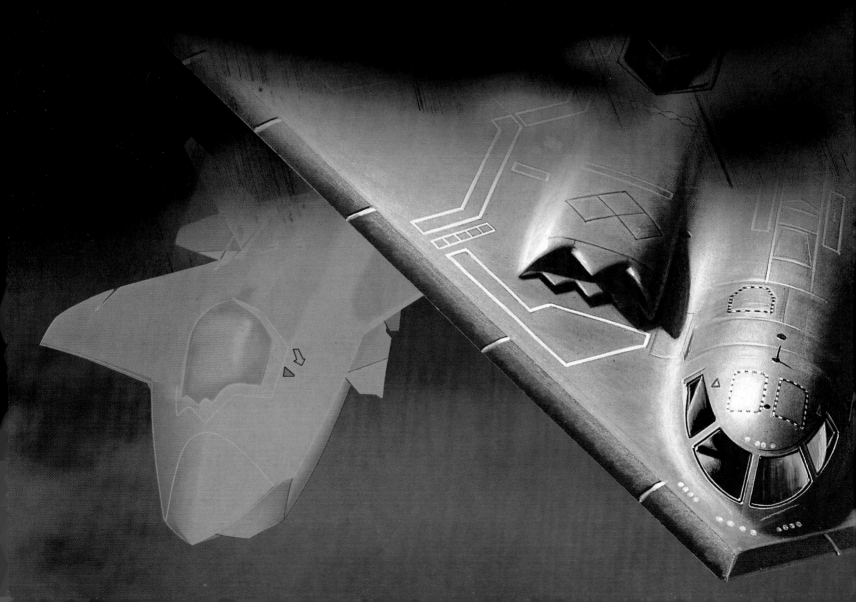

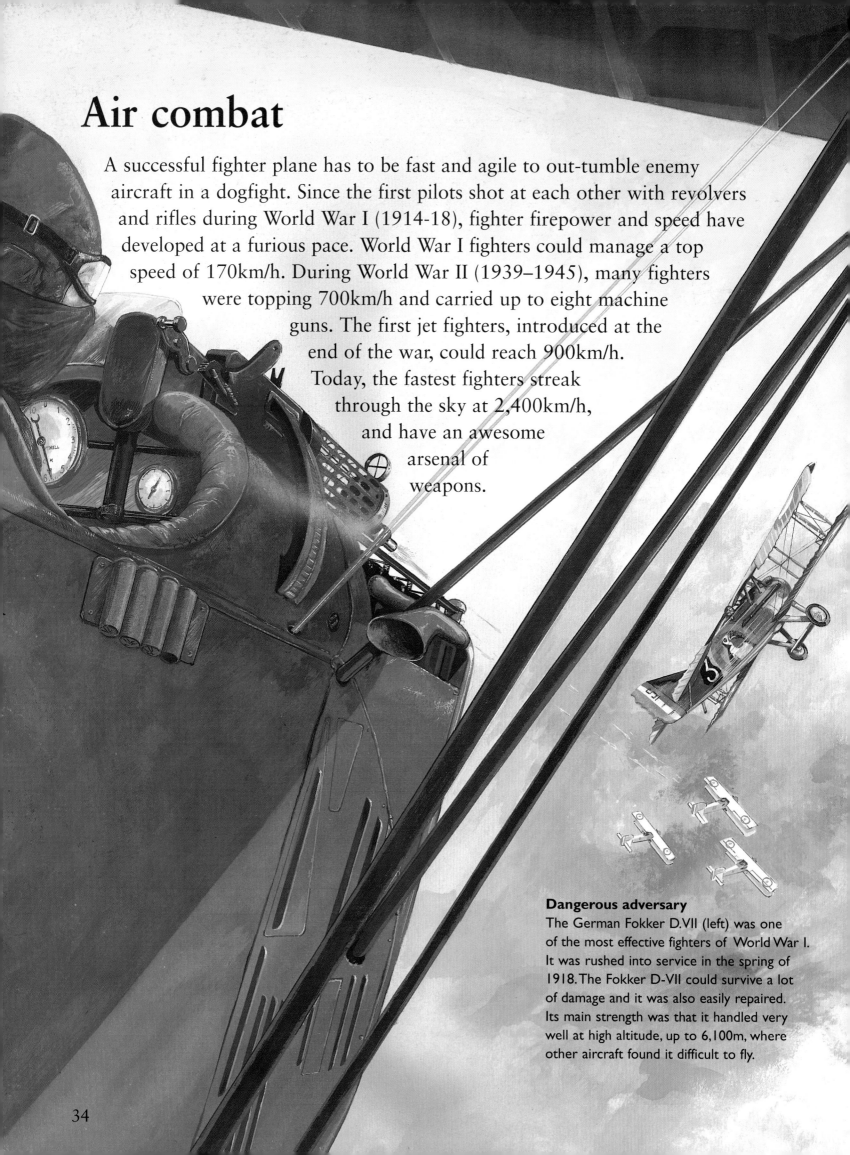

Air combat

A successful fighter plane has to be fast and agile to out-tumble enemy aircraft in a dogfight. Since the first pilots shot at each other with revolvers and rifles during World War I (1914-18), fighter firepower and speed have developed at a furious pace. World War I fighters could manage a top speed of 170km/h. During World War II (1939–1945), many fighters were topping 700km/h and carried up to eight machine guns. The first jet fighters, introduced at the end of the war, could reach 900km/h. Today, the fastest fighters streak through the sky at 2,400km/h, and have an awesome arsenal of weapons.

Dangerous adversary
The German Fokker D.VII (left) was one of the most effective fighters of World War I. It was rushed into service in the spring of 1918. The Fokker D-VII could survive a lot of damage and it was also easily repaired. Its main strength was that it handled very well at high altitude, up to 6,100m, where other aircraft found it difficult to fly.

Fighting for France

A French-built Spad S.13 (right) banks away from danger. A total of 8,472 Spad S.13s were built and flown by several air forces.

The Spitfire

The Supermarine Spitfire was the most important British fighter of World War II. More than 20,000 of them were built. It had a top speed of 720km/h and was armed with up to eight machine guns. With the Hawker Hurricane, the Spitfire helped Britain's pilots to win the Battle of Britain in 1940.

From machine guns to missiles

A faster fighter can close on its enemy and get out of trouble more quickly, but it cannot turn as tightly as a slower plane in a dogfight. As fighters have become faster, they have had to be able to attack each other from further away. Machine guns were a fighter's main weapon until the 1950s, when air-to-air missiles (AAMs) were introduced. Some of these missiles can now home in on a target up to 300km away from the attacking plane.

Fighting Falcon

The F-16 Fighting Falcon (left) was developed in the United States in the 1970s as a small, agile fighter for close combat. The F-16 has a wingspan of 10m, not much more than a World War I fighter, but it has a top speed of 2,146kph.

The Eurofighter

The Eurofighter EFA 2000 is being developed by Britain, Germany, Italy and Spain. Computers play a big part in operating the plane. The pilot can select a target just by looking at it and can activate a weapon by talking to the plane's computer.

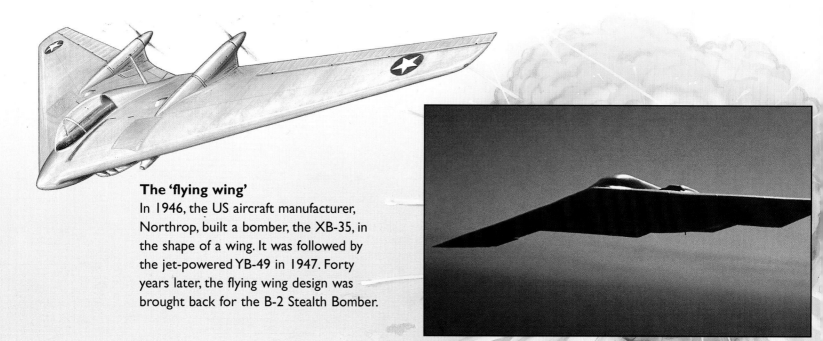

The 'flying wing'
In 1946, the US aircraft manufacturer, Northrop, built a bomber, the XB-35, in the shape of a wing. It was followed by the jet-powered YB-49 in 1947. Forty years later, the flying wing design was brought back for the B-2 Stealth Bomber.

Northrop B-2
The Northrop B-2 'Spirit' is also known as the Stealth Bomber. Guided by satellite, it is designed to get through enemy air defences without being detected and deliver up to 80 bombs or 16 missiles to key targets.

The black art of stealth

Stealth planes seem to appear out of nowhere and can surprise an enemy with devastating effect. These strangely shaped aircraft have a cloak of invisibility that allows them to slip through enemy radar undetected. Stealth planes such as the B-2 Stealth Bomber and the F-117 Nighthawk use special paint and materials to reduce radar reflections. Their carefully designed shape makes any remaining reflections bounce away from enemy radar systems.

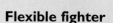

Flexible fighter
The Joint Strike Fighter is a multi-role stealth warplane being developed for the US Air Force, Navy and Marine Corps and the UK Royal Navy. The JSF will have short take-off and vertical landing ability and be able to climb one kilometre in five seconds. It is expected to enter service in 2008.

Iron-ball paint

One way of reducing radar reflections from an aircraft to make it more stealthy is to cover it with a special paint called iron-ball paint. This contains billions of microscopic iron balls that absorb radar signals. The balls allow the electric currents produced by the radar to flow through the paint, so less energy is reflected. Iron-ball paint is black when cold, but turns blue when it heats up during a flight.

DarkStar
DarkStar is an unpiloted spy-plane flown by remote control. It can fly at a height of over 13 kilometres and its shape makes it even stealthier than the F-117 or B-2.

F-117 Nighthawk
The F-117 Nighthawk is covered in flat panels that bounce radar signals away from an enemy transmitter. The engines' exhausts are broad and flat to make the hot gases mix well with the cool air and reduce the chance of heat detection.

Laser accuracy
The F-117 is armed with laser-guided bombs or missiles stored in two bays inside its body. When a weapon is released, a laser beam is fired at the target. The weapon locks onto the beam and flies to the target with pinpoint accuracy.

Dressing for action

Airline pilots and passengers fly in ordinary clothes, but military pilots and astronauts have to dress specially just to survive. A military pilot wears a helmet to protect the head in violent manoeuvres. An oxygen mask clips to the helmet. A G-suit, or partial pressure suit, fits over the flying suit. In tight turns, the G-suit inflates like a balloon around the lower half of the body, stopping blood from draining out of the head and pooling in the legs. Without the G-suit, the pilot would black out. Astronauts wear helmets and suits that completely cover their bodies, sealing them inside their own mini-atmosphere.

Wool and cork
In 1908, the American showman Samuel Franklin Cody made the first official powered flight in Britain. He wore a cork helmet, a thick woollen coat and leather boots.

Eye-tech helmet
This special helmet tracks eye movements, allowing an attack helicopter's pilot to aim weapons just by looking at the target. Information can also be projected onto the visor so that the pilot does not have to look down at the instrument panel.

Combat clothing
Every part of a military aircrew's clothing has a job to do. In addition to the helmet, oxygen mask, flight suit and G-suit, a life preserver is essential. If a landing in the sea is unavoidable, it inflates with gas to keep the crew member afloat.

Life-saver

Today, every fighter pilot wears a parachute. However, until the 1930s, many military flyers chose not to wear a parachute even though this meant that there was no escape from a crashing plane. Pilots believed that they had more chance of surviving by trying to land their plane than by trusting a flimsy piece of material. Attitudes changed just before World War II. During the war, about 100,000 airmen were saved by parachutes.

High-flyers

The crews of high-flying planes such as the Lockheed SR-71 Blackbird have to wear a helmet and full pressure suit similar to a spacesuit. The suit covers the whole body to protect the crew from the thin, freezing atmosphere.

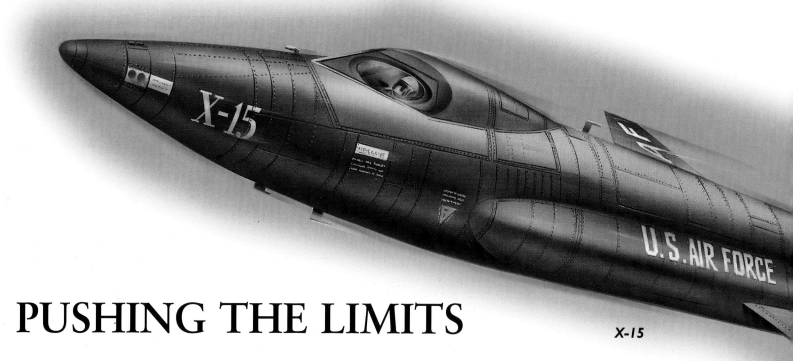

X-15

PUSHING THE LIMITS

Today, aircraft fly higher, faster and further than ever before. Advances in aircraft design depend on pioneering pilots, researchers and designers who are constantly pushing back the boundaries of aviation technology. The outer limits of an aircraft's performance are called its flight envelope. Test pilots fly every new aircraft to discover its flight envelope so that other pilots can fly it safely. When the Boeing 747 Jumbo Jet was designed, it underwent 1,500 hours of test flights using five aircraft over 10 months before it entered service with the world's airlines. Advances in aviation technology are often made by building experimental aircraft. These aircraft are not intended to go into production, but are built to test new developments.

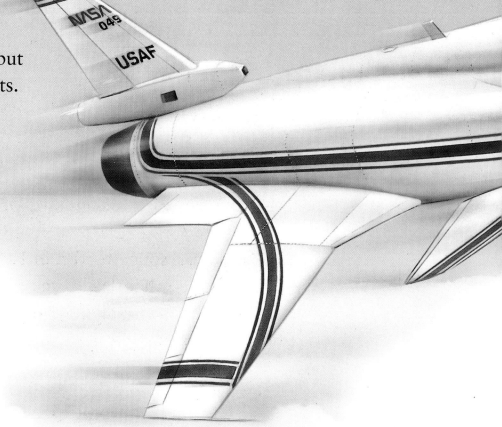

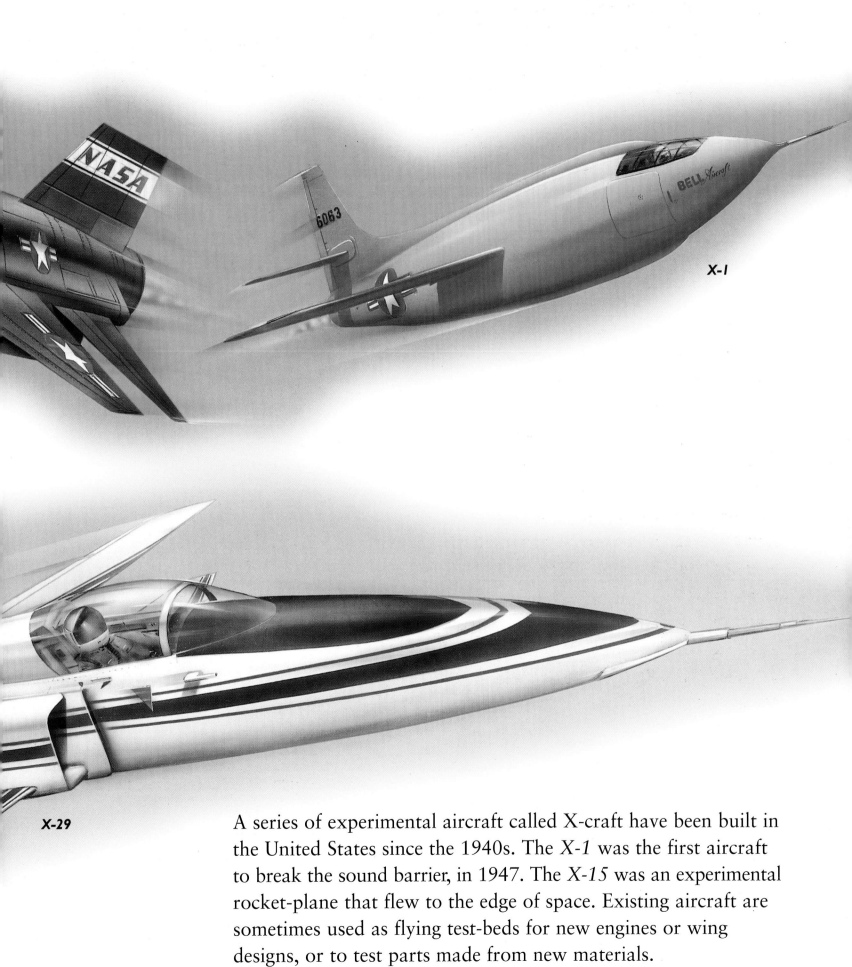

X-1

X-29

A series of experimental aircraft called X-craft have been built in the United States since the 1940s. The *X-1* was the first aircraft to break the sound barrier, in 1947. The *X-15* was an experimental rocket-plane that flew to the edge of space. Existing aircraft are sometimes used as flying test-beds for new engines or wing designs, or to test parts made from new materials.

The Wright brothers

On the morning of Thursday, December 17, 1903, Orville Wright lay down on the lower wing of the plane that he and his brother, Wilbur, had designed and built. The engine was started and the twin propellers spun up to speed. The plane accelerated along a wooden rail and rose into the air. It flew for 12 seconds and landed 36 metres away. The two brothers had made history. It was the first-ever controlled flight in a piloted machine taking off under its own power.

Otto Lilienthal

The German aviation pioneer Otto Lilienthal made more than 2,000 glider flights before he was killed in 1896 when his fixed-wing glider stalled. His work on controlling a wing in flight inspired other pioneers including the American brothers, Orville and Wilbur Wright.

Flyer No 2

By 1904, the Wright brothers were making routine flights of over five minutes. They built three different models called Flyer, then a two-seater model called the Type A.

Flight controls

The pilot of a Wright brothers' plane steered in two ways. He made the plane climb or dive by pulling a lever to tilt a pair of elevators at the front. He turned the plane by sliding to one side or the other. The pilot lay in a cradle linked to the wing-tips by wires. Sliding to one side moved the cradle and made one wing-tip twist one way while the other twisted the opposite direction. This made the plane roll into a turn. Later Wright planes had a seat for the pilot and the sliding cradle was replaced with a lever.

Making history
Orville Wright eases the first Flyer aeroplane into the air on Devember 17, 1903, at Kill Devil Hill, Kitty Hawk in North Carolina. Between them, Orville and Wilbur Wright made four flights that day, the longest lasting 59 seconds and covering almost 260 metres. It took another four years before European pioneers equalled this achievement.

Flying contraption
The Marquis d'Equevilly demonstrates his 'multiplane' in 1908. He mistakenly believed that aircraft should have as many wings as possible. After the Wright brothers' success in 1903, many pioneers in Europe attempted to build working aeroplanes.

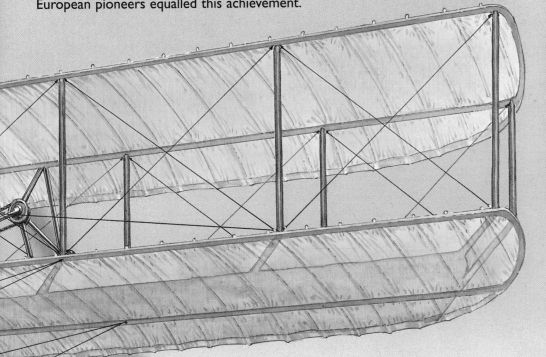

Flying the English Channel
On July 25, 1909, Louis Blériot made the first aeroplane flight across the Channel. He took off from Les Baraques, near Calais, in his Blériot XI aircraft and landed 36 minutes later at Northfall Meadow, near Dover.

The pioneers
By the 1920s, intrepid aviators had reached every continent. They proved that aeroplanes were a practical means of long-distance transport. The new air services that followed carried mail first, then passengers.

Trailblazers

Today, airline passengers and crew fly in comfort, protected by an array of navigation and safety systems. However, in the early years of flight, pilots often risked their lives trying to be the first to fly the routes that modern airliners use. From Louis Blériot's historic crossing of the Channel to Charles Lindbergh's epic journey across the Atlantic, pioneering flights were usually made in difficult and dangerous circumstances. This was the era of the great trailblazers – pilots whose ground-breaking flights played a key role in the development of aviation.

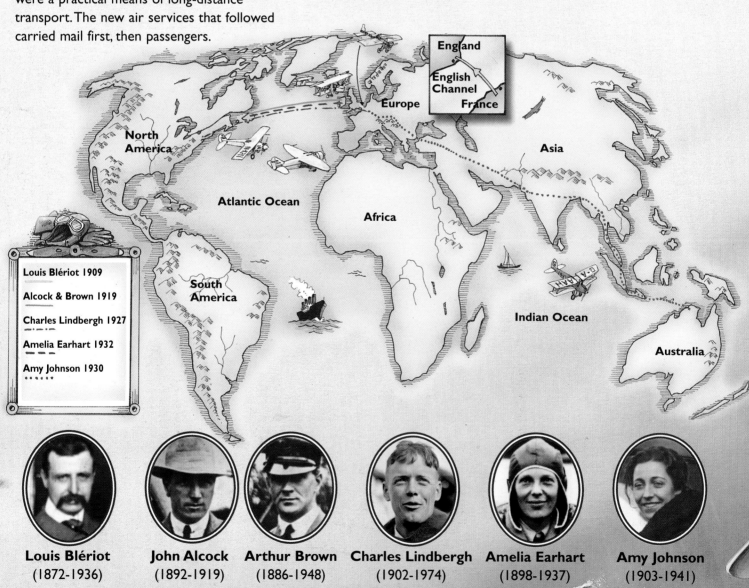

England
English Channel
France
Europe

North America

Asia

Atlantic Ocean

Africa

Louis Blériot 1909
Alcock & Brown 1919
Charles Lindbergh 1927
Amelia Earhart 1932
Amy Johnson 1930

South America

Indian Ocean

Australia

Louis Blériot
(1872-1936)

John Alcock
(1892-1919)

Arthur Brown
(1886-1948)

Charles Lindbergh
(1902-1974)

Amelia Earhart
(1898-1937)

Amy Johnson
(1903-1941)

The lure of the Atlantic

The greatest prize for early aviators was the North Atlantic, because it linked the most important business centres of the day – New York, London and Paris. An American Navy flying boat spanned the ocean in stages for the first time in May 1919. One month later, two Royal Air Force pilots, Captain John Alcock and Lieutenant Arthur Whitten Brown made the first non-stop flight across the North Atlantic. In a Vickers Vimy bomber, they took just under sixteen and a half hours to fly from St Johns, Newfoundland, to Clifden, in County Galway, Ireland.

A hero in the making
Charles Lindbergh's plane, *Spirit of St Louis*, skims the waves during the first non-stop solo flight across the Atlantic Ocean, in 1927. He took off from New York on May 20 and landed in Paris 33.5 hours later. The flight made him world-famous overnight.

Flying to fame
In 1932, Amelia Earhart was the first woman aviator to fly solo across the Atlantic Ocean. Three years later, she made the first solo flight from Hawaii to California. Tragically, she disappeared over the Pacific Ocean, in 1937, while trying to fly round the world.

Speed king

The world's fastest aircraft is the Lockheed SR-71 Blackbird. In 1976, it set a record speed of 3,530 km/h. The Blackbird was designed as a spy-plane that could fly so fast and so high that no enemy aircraft or missile could catch it or shoot it down. It had a crew of two. A pilot in the front cockpit flew the aircraft, while a navigator, who also operated the spying equipment, sat behind him. Today, the Blackbird is used for scientific research and testing high-speed propulsion systems.

In-flight refuelling
A Blackbird takes on fuel from a tanker plane. During a flight, a Blackbird has to be refuelled every two hours. NASA, the US aviation and space research agency, has two Blackbirds which carry out experiments at a height of more than 26,000 metres.

Top secret
A Blackbird accelerates to its tri-sonic (three times the speed of sound) cruising speed. The Blackbird was first flown in 1964. Missions usually lasted between two to five hours and its spy cameras could survey 260,000 km^2 of the Earth's surface every hour.

Dancing diamonds

Fiery 'dancing diamonds', caused by shockwaves in the engines' exhaust jets, stretch out behind a Blackbird as engine power is boosted to maximum.

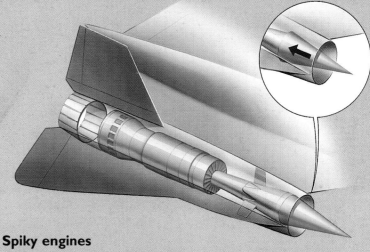

Spiky engines

The Blackbird's extremely powerful engines have a unique design. A spike at the front of each engine moves forwards or backwards to let in exactly the right amount of air.

Heat-resistant

The Blackbird flies so fast that air rushing past heats parts of the aircraft to temperatures of up to 500°C. Its outer skin is made almost entirely from titanium, a metal that can withstand very high temperatures without melting. The surface of the wings are crinkled. When a Blackbird is on the ground, you can see fuel leaking from gaps between the wing skins and their frames. But in the air, the wings flatten out and seal the gaps as metal expands when it heats up.

Parachute

A Blackbird touches down on the runway at 280 km/h and releases its braking parachute. This giant chute creates air resistance which helps the aircraft to slow down and come to a stop.

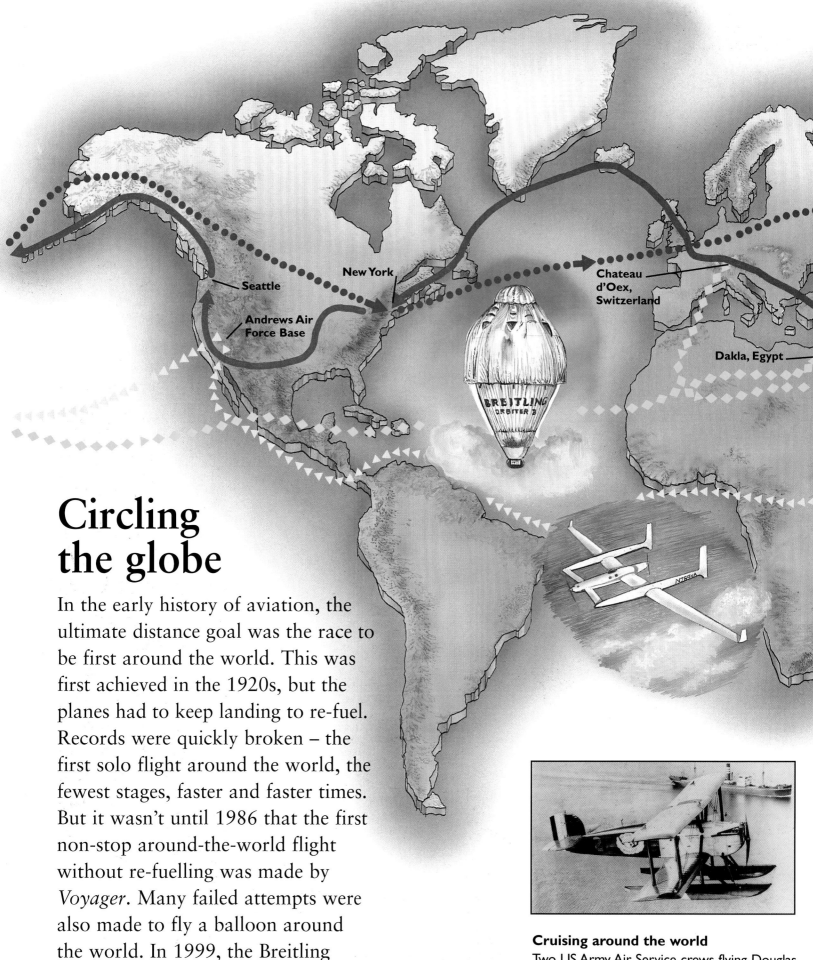

Seattle

New York

Andrews Air
Force Base

Chateau
d'Oex,
Switzerland

Dakla, Egypt

BREITLING
ORBITER 3

Circling the globe

In the early history of aviation, the ultimate distance goal was the race to be first around the world. This was first achieved in the 1920s, but the planes had to keep landing to re-fuel. Records were quickly broken – the first solo flight around the world, the fewest stages, faster and faster times. But it wasn't until 1986 that the first non-stop around-the-world flight without re-fuelling was made by *Voyager*. Many failed attempts were also made to fly a balloon around the world. In 1999, the Breitling *Orbiter 3* balloon finally succeeded and set the last great aviation record of the 20th century.

Cruising around the world
Two US Army Air Service crews flying Douglas World Cruiser single-engined biplanes made the very first around-the-world flight in 1924. They made the trip in 175 days and covered 44,340km, with 72 stops on the way.

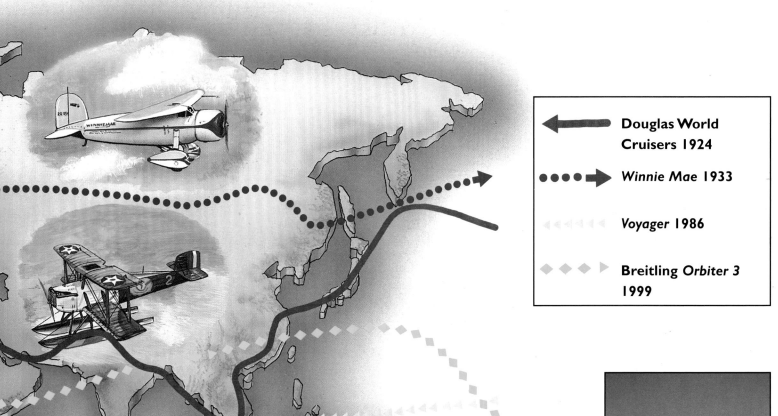

⬅	**Douglas World Cruisers** 1924
●●●●➤	*Winnie Mae* 1933
◄◄◄◄◄	*Voyager* 1986
◆◆◆▶	**Breitling** *Orbiter 3* 1999

Lucky Lady

The first non-stop around-the-world flight was achieved in 1949 by the US Air Force. A Boeing B-50 Superfortress, called *Lucky Lady II*, made the 37,740km flight in 93 hours. The aircraft had to be re-fuelled in the air four times. In-flight re-fuelling was specially devised for this record-breaking flight.

Wiley Post

The first solo around-the-world flight was made in 1933 by the American pilot Wiley Post. He flew his Lockheed Vega, called *Winnie Mae*, 25,099km in less than eight days, starting and finishing at New York, USA.

Voyager

The first non-stop around-the-world flight without refuelling was made by Dick Rutan and Jeana Yeager in 1986. The 40,212km flight took place in their experimental aeroplane, *Voyager*, in just over nine days.

Breitling *Orbiter 3*

The Breitling *Orbiter 3* balloon with Bertrand Piccard and Brian Jones on-board took advantage of a high-altitude wind, or jet stream, to float 48,000km around the world in 19 days.

Rocket pioneer
Robert Goddard
(1882–1945) launched the
first liquid-fuelled rocket, in
the United States in 1926. It
burned gasoline fuel mixed
with liquid oxygen.

Saturn V
The giant Saturn V rocket
was built to send Apollo
spacecraft to the Moon. It
had three stages, stood
110.6m tall and weighed
more than 2,700 tonnes.

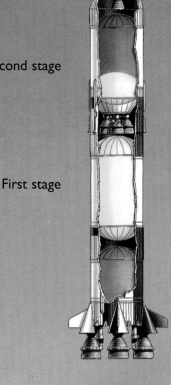

Third stage

Second stage

First stage

Beyond the atmosphere

A new chapter in the story of flight began when the
Soviet Union launched the first artificial satellite,
Sputnik 1, in 1957, and the first man into space
in 1961. They were launched on top of rockets, the
only engines powerful enough to blast a payload into
orbit and work beyond the atmosphere. The United
States and Soviet Union competed in a space race to
put a person on the Moon. In July 1969, the US
Apollo 11 mission landed the first
astronauts there. Today's
space vehicles, such as the
space shuttle, are still
propelled by rockets.

Shuttle mission
The space shuttle takes off like a rocket but
lands like a glider on a runway. The first space
shuttle, *Columbia*, was launched in 1981.

Rocket plane

Neil Armstrong, who later became the first person to set foot on the Moon, stands in front of the experimental rocket-plane, the *X-15*. Between 1959 and 1968 it made scores of flights to the edge of the atmosphere.

Resisting heat

The space shuttle orbiter re-enters the atmosphere at 26,000km/h – or twenty-five times the speed of sound. Friction between the orbiter and the air rushing past create extremely high temperatures. The space shuttle is covered with 20,000 heat-resistant glass tiles. The hottest parts of the shuttle, the nose and front edges of the wing are made from carbon and designed to withstand temperatures of 1,260°C.

Blast-off
At blast-off, the space shuttle's three main engines and two booster rockets provide thrust equivalent to 140 Jumbo Jets.

Flying into the future

Aircraft have developed at an astonishing pace since the Wright brothers made the first-ever aeroplane flight in 1903. The first supersonic flight, for example, came only 44 years later. In the near future, aircraft are set to become faster and even larger. The first 'super-jumbo' airliner is expected to enter service in 2005. And in 30 years time, there may be rocket planes carrying passengers at more than ten times the speed of sound and flying so high that they skim the top of the atmosphere.

Experimental space-plane

If spaceflight is to become commonplace, new space-planes will have to be less expensive to launch. The *X-33* was designed as a half-size prototype for one of these craft. The project was cancelled by NASA in 2001, but future space-planes will benefit from the research that went into it.

United States

NASA

LOCKHEED MAR

Hypersoar

By 2035, Hypersoar may be transporting passengers and cargo at speeds of up to 10,000km/h. Hypersoar is designed to skip across the top of the atmosphere. As Hypersoar sinks back into the atmosphere, a burst of engine power boosts it to the right height again. This unique trajectory will protect Hypersoar from excessive overheating in the atmosphere.

Faster airliners

Airliner passengers want to get to their destinations as fast as possible, so a research group in the United States is developing a new supersonic airliner for the 21st century. The High Speed Civil Transport (HSCT) will halve flight times between the United States and the Far East or Europe. It will carry up to 300 passengers at mach 2.4 (2.4 times the speed of sound). Its designers are developing new engines for it that will be as quiet as today's subsonic airliner engines. A flight in the HSCT from Los Angeles, USA, to Tokyo, Japan, will be six hours shorter than a normal subsonic flight. An HSCT flight in stages from Los Angeles to Sydney, Australia, would save 10 hours on a subsonic flight today.

Super-jumbo

The European aircraft manufacturer, Airbus Industrie, is developing the world's biggest airliner. The Airbus A3XX, which is now known as the A380, is a giant airliner that will carry 555 passengers in three classes or up to 900 people in an all-economy class layout. The A380 will be assembled in France; its parts will be built there as well as in Britain, Germany and Spain.

Future airport

Tiltrotor aircraft for short-haul flights will be a common sight at airports by 2010. Airports will need to evolve to meet the needs of new kinds of aircraft as well as coping with the rise in air passenger numbers. Automated passenger handling systems such as passport control and security will reduce waiting time on the ground and prevent overcrowding.

X-33

Controlling an aircraft

Aeroplanes are able to fly because of the shape of their wings. Air flows faster over the curved top than across the flat underside. This creates a force called lift, which pulls the aircraft upwards. An aeroplane is steered by moving panels called control surfaces. There are three types – ailerons in the wings, and elevators and rudder in the tail.

Steering
A plane is steered in three ways – pitch, roll and yaw. Changing its pitch brings the nose up or down. Rolling it brings one wing up and the other down. Yaw turns the nose to the left or right.

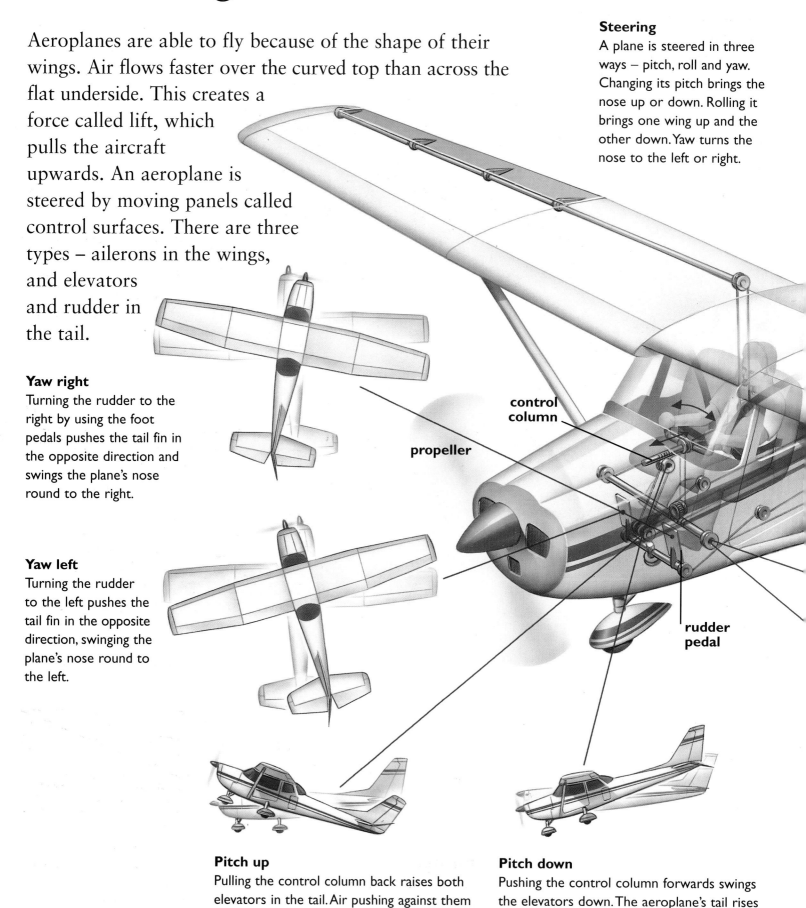

Yaw right
Turning the rudder to the right by using the foot pedals pushes the tail fin in the opposite direction and swings the plane's nose round to the right.

Yaw left
Turning the rudder to the left pushes the tail fin in the opposite direction, swinging the plane's nose round to the left.

control column

propeller

rudder pedal

Pitch up
Pulling the control column back raises both elevators in the tail. Air pushing against them presses the tail down and brings the nose up.

Pitch down
Pushing the control column forwards swings the elevators down. The aeroplane's tail rises and its nose tips downwards.

Turning

An aeroplane turns by raising one wing and lowering the other. Sideways pull swings the plane into a turn. The elevators and rudder are used to make small adjustments to keep the aeroplane level and pointing in the right direction during the turn.

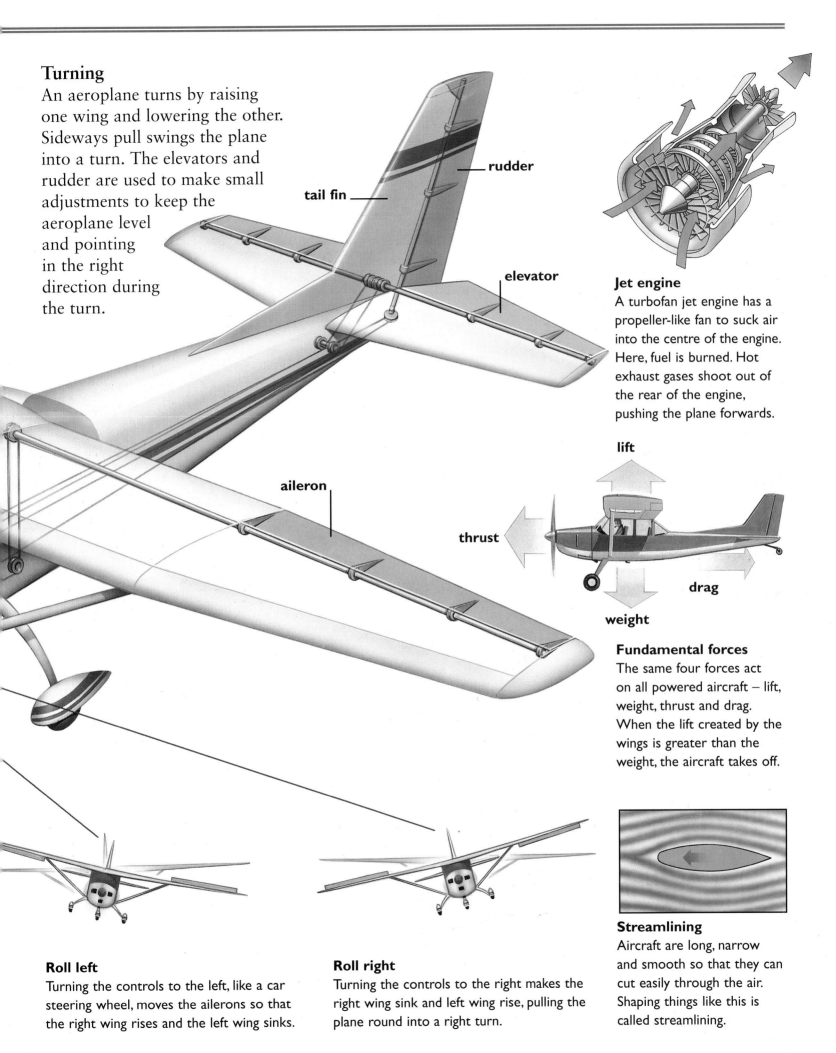

rudder

tail fin

elevator

aileron

Jet engine
A turbofan jet engine has a propeller-like fan to suck air into the centre of the engine. Here, fuel is burned. Hot exhaust gases shoot out of the rear of the engine, pushing the plane forwards.

lift

thrust

drag

weight

Fundamental forces
The same four forces act on all powered aircraft – lift, weight, thrust and drag. When the lift created by the wings is greater than the weight, the aircraft takes off.

Streamlining
Aircraft are long, narrow and smooth so that they can cut easily through the air. Shaping things like this is called streamlining.

Roll left
Turning the controls to the left, like a car steering wheel, moves the ailerons so that the right wing rises and the left wing sinks.

Roll right
Turning the controls to the right makes the right wing sink and left wing rise, pulling the plane round into a right turn.

55

The plane facts

From the smallest microlight to the biggest airliner, every type of aircraft has a unique set of personal statistics. These include its wingspan, length and speed. On these pages you will find a selection of aircraft types, all pictured to scale. The huge variation in size, shape and performance reflects the wide range of roles for which different aircraft are designed.

Concorde
Speed: 2,333km/h
Passengers: up to 144
Flight crew: 3
Length: 62.1m
Wingspan: 25.6m

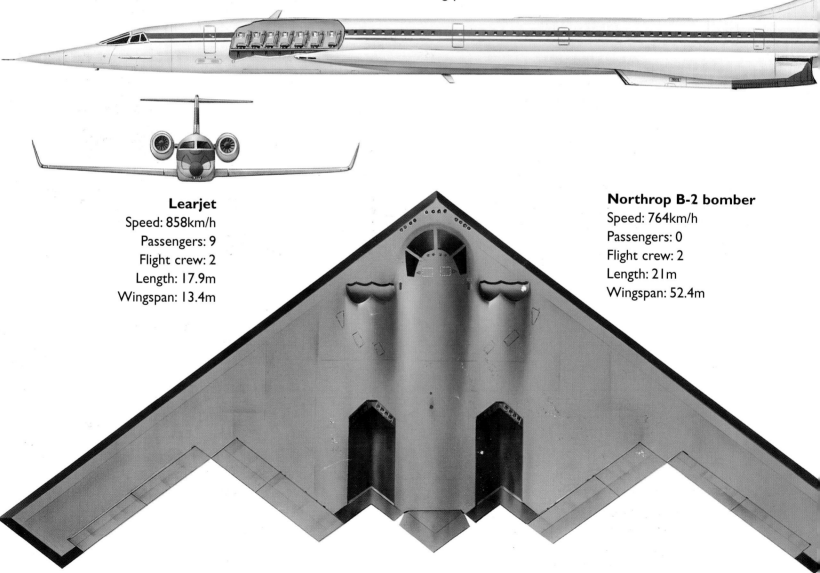

Learjet
Speed: 858km/h
Passengers: 9
Flight crew: 2
Length: 17.9m
Wingspan: 13.4m

Northrop B-2 bomber
Speed: 764km/h
Passengers: 0
Flight crew: 2
Length: 21m
Wingspan: 52.4m

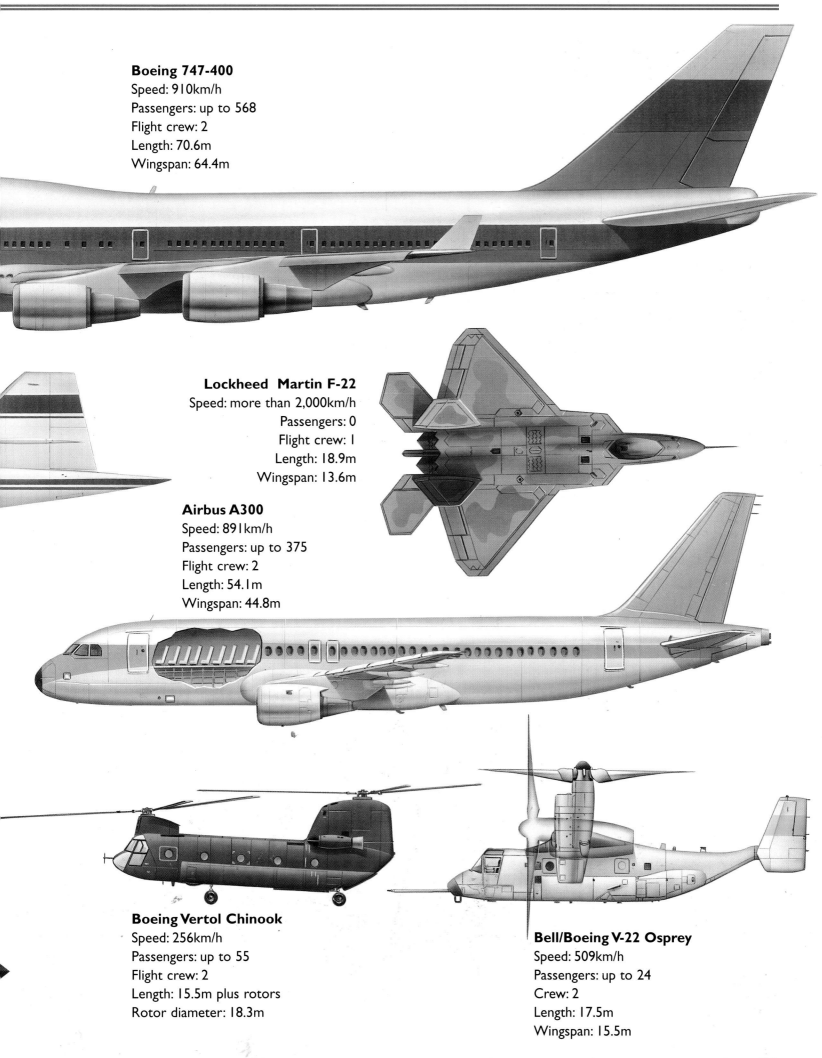

Boeing 747-400
Speed: 910km/h
Passengers: up to 568
Flight crew: 2
Length: 70.6m
Wingspan: 64.4m

Lockheed Martin F-22
Speed: more than 2,000km/h
Passengers: 0
Flight crew: 1
Length: 18.9m
Wingspan: 13.6m

Airbus A300
Speed: 891km/h
Passengers: up to 375
Flight crew: 2
Length: 54.1m
Wingspan: 44.8m

Boeing Vertol Chinook
Speed: 256km/h
Passengers: up to 55
Flight crew: 2
Length: 15.5m plus rotors
Rotor diameter: 18.3m

Bell/Boeing V-22 Osprey
Speed: 509km/h
Passengers: up to 24
Crew: 2
Length: 17.5m
Wingspan: 15.5m

Flying firsts

Most modern aircraft can trace their ancestry back to the Wright Flyer. New aircraft generally improve on existing models in small ways. They might be a little bit bigger or fly a little faster or higher. But from time to time, innovations or breakthroughs are made that transform aircraft technology. For instance, when Frank Whittle invented the jet engine in the 1940s, it revolutionized air transport. And when Wernher von Braun and Sergei Korolev developed the world's biggest rockets after World War II, they made manned spaceflight possible.

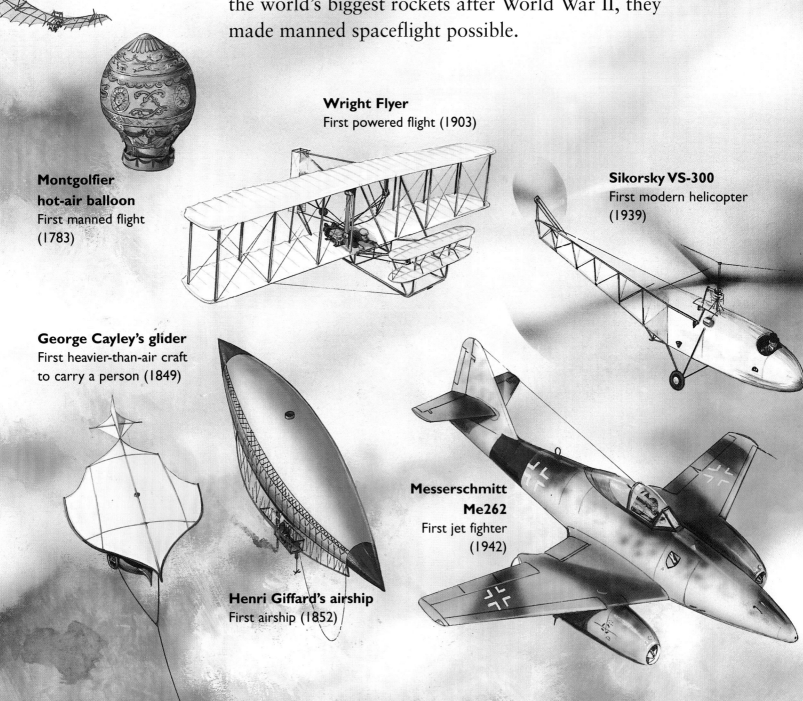

Leonardo da Vinci's drawings of flying machines
(1480s-1500)

Montgolfier hot-air balloon
First manned flight
(1783)

Wright Flyer
First powered flight (1903)

Sikorsky VS-300
First modern helicopter
(1939)

George Cayley's glider
First heavier-than-air craft to carry a person (1849)

Messerschmitt Me262
First jet fighter
(1942)

Henri Giffard's airship
First airship (1852)

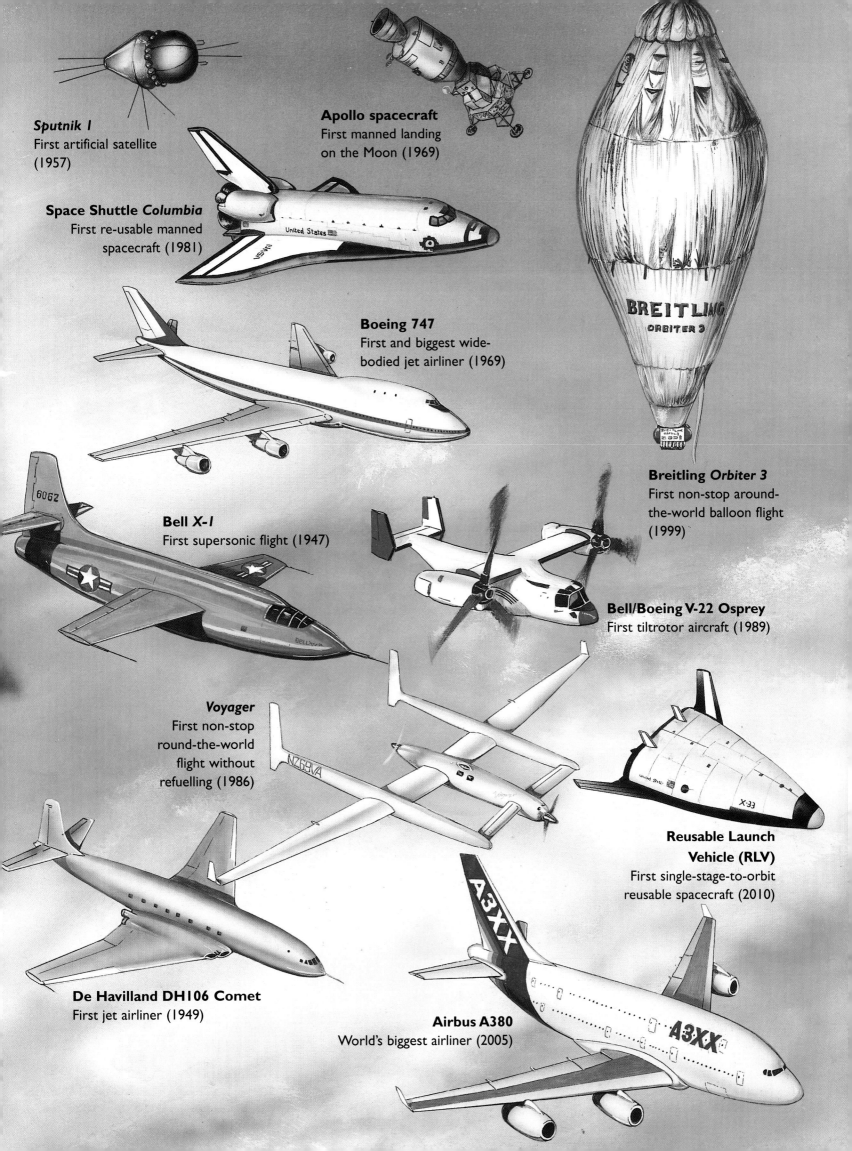

Sputnik 1
First artificial satellite
(1957)

Apollo spacecraft
First manned landing
on the Moon (1969)

Space Shuttle *Columbia*
First re-usable manned
spacecraft (1981)

Boeing 747
First and biggest wide-
bodied jet airliner (1969)

Breitling *Orbiter 3*
First non-stop around-
the-world balloon flight
(1999)

Bell *X-1*
First supersonic flight (1947)

Bell/Boeing V-22 Osprey
First tiltrotor aircraft (1989)

Voyager
First non-stop
round-the-world
flight without
refuelling (1986)

**Reusable Launch
Vehicle (RLV)**
First single-stage-to-orbit
reusable spacecraft (2010)

De Havilland DH106 Comet
First jet airliner (1949)

Airbus A380
World's biggest airliner (2005)

Glossary

aeroplane A powered, heavier-than-air craft.

ailerons Control surfaces in a plane's wings that tilt to make the plane roll to one side or the other.

air traffic control An organization that guides aircraft through the sky by monitoring their position using radar and giving pilots instructions by radio.

airframe The basic structure of an aircraft, not including its engines.

airship A powered, lighter-than-air craft.

altitude The height of an aircraft above sea level.

atmosphere The air that surrounds the Earth.

biplane A plane with two sets of wings, one above the other.

black boxes Another name for the flight data recorder and the cockpit voice recorder. These two recorders are carried in airliners to provide clues to the cause of an accident.

blind flying Flying by using instruments only, because the view outside an aircraft has disappeared due to fog or cloud, or because it is dark.

civil aviation Non-military flying.

cockpit The part of an aircraft where the pilot sits.

cockpit voice recorder (CVR) One of two recorders carried in an airliner. The CVR records everything the pilots say and can give vital clues if an accident happens.

combustion chamber The part of an engine where the fuel is burned.

control surfaces A set of movable panels on an aircraft that are moved by the pilot to make the aircraft climb, turn and dive.

dirigible Another name for an airship.

dogfight Close combat between fighter planes as they chase each other and try to shoot each other down.

drag Another name for air resistance, or the tendency of air to slow down anything that tries to fly through it.

ejector seat A seat in a fighter plane that blasts the pilot to safety in an emergency. Once clear of the aircraft, the pilot lands by parachute.

elevators Control surfaces in a plane's tail that tilt to make the tail rise or fall. This makes the plane dive or climb.

elevon A control surface used by delta-wing planes that works as both an elevator and aileron.

fixed-wing aircraft Aircraft with wings that do not move, unlike helicopters which have spinning rotors.

flaps Panels that slide out from the aeroplane's wings to make them bigger. This helps provide more lift when the plane is flying slowly after take-off and before landing.

flight data recorder One of the two recorders carried by an airliner to give clues to the cause of an accident. The other recorder is the cockpit voice recorder.

flight deck The part of a large aircraft, such as an airliner, where the crew sits.

flight envelope The range of speeds and heights within which an aircraft can fly safely.

flight simulator A copy of an aircraft's cockpit or flight deck used to train and test pilots. The simulator moves and the pilots see computer-generated views to make 'flying' the simulator as realistic as possible.

float plane Another name for a seaplane.

flying boat A plane with a watertight, boat-shaped hull designed to land in water.

flying wing A plane shaped like a large wing.

fuselage Another name for the main body of a plane.

G-suit A tight suit worn by a fighter pilot. The suit inflates like a balloon to squeeze the pilot's lower body and legs to stop blood draining away from the head during tight turns.

gas turbine Another name for the jet engine, a turbine engine driven by gas. The gas is produced by burning fuel inside the engine.

glider An unpowered fixed-wing aircraft.

global positioning system (GPS) A navigation system that enables pilots and others to locate their position very accurately by using radio signals from satellites.

hangar A building where aircraft are housed and stored.

hang-glider A basic unpowered aircraft made from a wing, from which the pilot hangs and steers by moving his or her body.

helipad An open space set aside for helicopters to land and take off.

landing gear An aircraft's wheels, or undercarriage.

lift A upwards-acting force produced by an aircraft that enables it to take off and fly. Lift can be produced by wings, rotor blades, engine thrust or a lighter-than-air gas.

lighter-than-air (LTA) craft Aircraft that produce lift by carrying a large bag of gas such as hot air, hydrogen or helium that is lighter than the surrounding air.

microburst A strong wind blowing downwards from the base of a thunderstorm. A microburst can cause a sudden change in wind direction called windshear.

microlight A small lightweight leisure aircraft, often with an open cockpit, capable of carrying one or two people.

monoplane A fixed-wing aircraft with one wing across the top or on each side.

navigation Steering a course to find the way from one place to another.

piston engine A type of engine used by the smallest planes and helicopters that works like a car engine. Fuel burned inside cylinders forces pistons down the cylinders to turn a propeller or rotor.

pitch A movement of an aircraft that tilts its nose up or down.

pylon A post fixed to an aircraft's wing for attaching an engine. Combat planes and bombers also have pylons under their wings for carrying weapons.

radar A system for locating aircraft by sending out bursts of radio signals and detecting any reflections that bounce back.

retractable wheels Wheels that fold up inside an aircraft when it takes off.

rocket A vehicle propelled by one or more rocket motors.

rocket motor An engine that produces thrust like a jet engine. The rocket engine carries its own supply of oxygen to enable it to burn its fuel without any need to take in air.

roll The banking movement of an aircraft in which one wing rises and the other falls.

rotor A set of rotating wing-shaped blades. A spinning rotor provides lift for a helicopter.

rotorcraft An aircraft powered by one or more rotors, such as a helicopter.

rudder A control surface in an aircraft's tail fin that swivels to the left or right to turn the plane in a particular direction.

satellite An object that circles a planet. The Moon is a natural satellite of the Earth. A spacecraft orbiting the Earth is an artificial satellite.

seaplane A plane fitted with floats so that it can land on water. It is sometimes also called a float plane.

speed of sound The speed at which sound travels. It varies according to air temperature. At sea level, it is about 1,125km/h. At higher altitudes, where it is colder, the speed of sound drops to about 1,060km/h.

stealth plane A military plane that is designed to be difficult to detect by radar.

subsonic Slower than the speed of sound.

supersonic Faster than the speed of sound.

tailplane The small wing-like panels in the tail of an aircraft.

thermal A rising current of warm air. Thermals are used by glider pilots to climb higher. A glider circling inside a thermal is carried upwards with the rising air.

thrust The force produced by an aircraft's engine or a rocket motor to make an aircraft or spacecraft move.

turbofan An efficient type of jet engine that has a large spinning fan at the front to suck air into the engine.

turboprop A type of jet engine that drives a propeller.

windshear A sudden change in wind direction.

yaw A turn to the left or right.

Index

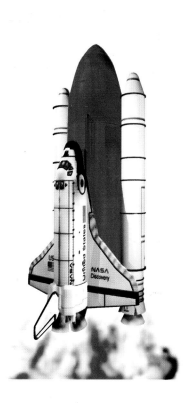

Acknowledgements

The publishers would like to thank the following
illustrators for their contributions to this book:
b = bottom, c = centre, l = left, r = right, t = top, m = middle
Julian Baker 8 *m*, 21 *tr*, 26–27, 29 *tr* 50 *tr*; **Julian Baum** 52 *bl*; **Mark Bergin** 1 *c*, 12–13, 14–15, 16–17,
18–19, 20–21, 24–25, 36–37, 44–45; **Nick Clifford** 53 *mr*; **Tom Connell** cover, 4–5, 28–29, 32–33, 50–51;
Sidney Coulridge 30–31; **Mike Davis** 32 *bl*; **Alan Hancocks** 10–11, 22–23, 40–41, 46–47, 54–55, 56–57;
John James 38–39, 42–43; **B Knight** 33 *mr*; **Chris Lion** 22 *tl*; **Kevin Maddison** 6–7, 8–9, 27*tl*, 34–35, 48–49,
58–59; **David Russell** 55 *tr*.

The publishers would also like to thank the following for supplying photographs for this book:
6 *tr* TRH; **7** *t* Quadrant Picture Library; **8** *tl* Quadrant Picture Library, *br* Science Photo Library/Philippe
Gontier/Eurelios/Onera; **11** *tc* Quadrant Picture Library/Simon Everett; **12** *t* Corbis; *c* TRH; **14** *cl* Corbis; **15** *tc* Corbis;
c TRH/Canadair; **16** *t* Hulton Getty; **18** *cl* TRH/R Winslade; **19** *t* Science & Society Picture Library/George
Woodbine/Daily Herald Archive/NMPFT, *tr* TRH; **20** *tl* Corbis; **21** *tl* Corbis, *br* The Aviation Picture Library; **22** *br*
Popperfoto; **25** *tr* NASA; **26** *br* Corbis; **28** *tl* Royal Aeronautical Society, *cl* The Aviation Picture Library; **29** *c* Quadrant
Picture Library *b*, Topham Picture Point; **30** *tl* Royal Aeronautical Society, *bc* Royal Aeronautical Society; **35** *tr*
Quadrant Picture Library *cr*, TRH/British Aerospace; **36** *tr* Quadrant Picture Library/Erik Simonsen, 1994, *bl* The
Aviation Picture Library/Northrop Grumman; **37** *tr* The Aviation Picture Library; **38** *tl* Science & Society Picture
Library/Science Museum, *bl* The Aviation Picture Library/Patrick Darphin; **39** *tr* NASA; **42** *tl* TRH//Munich Museum; **43**
tl Science Photo Library/US Library of Congress, *cr* Hulton Getty; **44** *bl* (centre) Science & Society Picture
Library/Daily Herald Archive/NMPFT, *bl* Corbis/Underwood & Underwood *bc* Corbis *br* Science & Society Picture
Library/DHA/NMPFT; **45** *tc* The Aviation Picture Library; **46** *cl* NASA; **47** *b* NASA; **48** *br* Royal Aeronautical Society;
49 *r* The Aviation Picture Library, *bl* The Aviation Picture Library, *bc* Rex Features; **50** *tc* Science Photo Library/NASA;
51 *tl* NASA; **52–53** *c* NASA; **53** *tr* Rex Features.

Every effort has been made to trace the copyright holders of the photographs.
The publishers apologise for any inconvenience caused.

Below is a list of useful websites:
www.nasm.edu (Smithsonian National Air & Space Museum)
www.iwm.org.uk/duxford.htm (Imperial War Museum, Duxford)
www.rafmuseum.org.uk (RAF Museum, Hendon)
www.nasa.gov (NASA aviation and space site)
http://x33.msfc.nasa.gov (NASA details of the *X33* re-usable spaceplane)
www.bhpa.co.uk (British Hang-gliding Pilots Association)
www.avnet.co.uk/bmaa (British Microlight Aircraft Association)
www.gliding.co.uk (British Gliding Association)
www.aloha.net/~icarus (Aloha Flight 243 accident)
spaceflight.nasa.gov (Space Shuttle/Space Station)